T0194034

I AM LIGHT - LOVE - LIFE!

"Who is Jesus Christ?"

MICHAEL HUNTER

authorHOUSE

AuthorHouse™
1663 Liberty Drive
Bloomington, IN 47403
www.authorhouse.com
Phone: 833-262-8899

© 2020 Michael Hunter. All rights reserved.

No part of this book may be reproduced, stored in a retrieval system, or transmitted by any means without the written permission of the author.

Published by AuthorHouse 07/25/2020

ISBN: 978-1-7283-6609-8 (sc)
ISBN: 978-1-7283-6608-1 (e)

Print information available on the last page.

Any people depicted in stock imagery provided by Getty Images are models, and such images are being used for illustrative purposes only. Certain stock imagery © Getty Images.

This book is printed on acid-free paper.

Because of the dynamic nature of the Internet, any web addresses or links contained in this book may have changed since publication and may no longer be valid. The views expressed in this work are solely those of the author and do not necessarily reflect the views of the publisher, and the publisher hereby disclaims any responsibility for them.

Scripture quotations marked NLT are taken from the Holy Bible, New Living Translation, copyright © 1996, 2004, 2007. Used by permission of Tyndale House Publishers, Inc. Carol Stream, Illinois 60188. All rights reserved. Website

Scripture quotations marked KJV are from the Holy Bible, King James Version (Authorized Version). First published in 1611. Quoted from the KJV Classic Reference Bible, Copyright © 1983 by The Zondervan Corporation.

Scripture quotations marked MSG are taken from THE MESSAGE. Copyright © 1993, 1994, 1995, 1996, 2000, 2001, 2002, 2003 by Eugene H. Peterson. Used by permission of NavPress Publishing Group. Website.

Scripture quotations marked NKJV are taken from the New King James Version. Copyright © 1982 by Thomas Nelson, Inc. Used by permission. All rights reserved.

Scripture quotations have all been taken from online Bible Search website:

"Bible Gateway" https://www.biblegateway.com as per the following information.

Scriptures marked KJV are taken from the *King James Version,* Public Domain; Scriptures marked NLT are taken from the New Living Translation, copyright ©1996, 2004, 2015 by Tyndale House Foundation. Used by permission of Tyndale House Publishers Inc., Carol Stream Illinois 60188. All rights reserved. Scriptures marked NIV are taken from *The Holy Bible, New International Version*, Copyright ©1973, 1974, 1978, 1984, 2011 by Biblica, Inc.® Used by permission. All rights reserved worldwide. Scriptures marked NKJV are taken from *New King James Version* (NKJV) Copyright ©1982 by Thomas Nelson. Used by permission. All rights reserved. Scriptures marked MSG are taken from *The Message,* Copyright ©1993, 1994, 1995, 1996, 2000, 2001, 2002 by Eugene H. Peterson. All rights reserved.

CONTENTS

INTRODUCTION

In the Bible, the Apostle John, gives us a wonderful description of God's true nature, saying:

> But anyone who does not love does not know God, for God is love. God showed how much he loved us by sending his one and only Son into the world so that we might have eternal life through him. This is real love—not that we loved God, but that he loved us and sent his Son as a sacrifice to take away our sins. 1 John 4:8-10 NLT

Yes, God is the embodiment of love, real love. He was so loving that He suffered the sacrifice of His only Son so that we could be saved. The truth is that God does not want anyone to perish. God does not want anyone in hell. Hell was not even created with the desire for humans to inhabit it. This place of eternal fire was specifically designed to be the final destination of the Devil and his angels, and only those who follow Satan will go there, to God's regret (see Matthew 25:41 KJV). Yet, is this the God described in many churches today?

Unfortunately, non-believers and a sizeable number of professing Christians are determined to misrepresent God to mankind as an angry and vengeful Deity who slaughters the innocent and delights in the death of the wicked. Is that who God is to you? If so, I will let God reveal the truth to you in His own words:

> As surely as I live, says the Sovereign Lord, I take no pleasure in the death of wicked people. I only want them to turn from their wicked ways so they can live. Turn!

Turn from your wickedness, O people of Israel! Why should you die? Ezekiel 33:11 NLT

So if God is not the vengeful killer and murderer of innocents that people accuse Him of being, then who is He? Just as important, if God is not the one who steals, kills and destroys, then who is the one who is really behind all of the evil in the world?

Did you know that the English word "Satan" comes from the Hebrew and Greek words meaning "accuser, attacker, and adversary"? Did you know that the English word "Devil" comes from the Hebrew and Greek words meaning "slanderer, false accuser, and devastator"? The Bible explains to us that Satan is a real spiritual being, and John 8:44 KJV exposes Satan as a liar, declaring to us that he was a murderer from the beginning.

As you read this book, I hope and pray that you will hear God's heart as the Holy Spirit shines light in the darkness. I hope you will allow the Spirit of God to open your understanding of who is the real destroyer of the human race, and who is our loving Father in Heaven and beloved Savior. I pray that the Lord will be with you as you learn from His Word that GOD IS LIGHT, GOD IS LOVE and GOD IS LIFE.

GOD IS LIGHT

…I am the light of the world… (John 8:12 KJV)

And this is the condemnation, that light is come into the world, and men loved darkness rather than light, because their deeds were evil. (John 3:19 KJV)

GOD IS LOVE

This is real love—not that we loved God, but that he loved us and sent his Son as a sacrifice to take away our sins. (1 John 4:10 NLT)

GOD IS LIFE

And this is the record that God hath given to us eternal life, and this life is in his Son. (1John 5:11 KJV)

Jesus saith unto him, I am the way, the truth, and the life. No man cometh unto the Father, but by me. (John 14:6 KJV)

CHAPTER 1

Who Really Killed Adam and Eve?

CHRIST OVERCAME THE CORRUPTED WORD OF GOD WITH THE TRUE WORD OF GOD.

Many people do not realize how vitally important it is to study and know the Word of God in these end-times we live in. The truth is that our God is a wonderful miracle-working, kind and compassionate God.

The way to salvation is a straight and simple path according to the Word of God. Repent, and believe on the Lord Jesus Christ. However, sometimes in our efforts to share the gospel, Christians will discover that many of the people we are trying to reach are struggling with deeper questions about God and the Bible that are not directly connected to salvation, yet their lack of accurate knowledge of God's Word is hindering them from coming to a place of faith in God. For their sakes, God tells us:

...you must worship Christ as Lord of your life. And if someone asks about your hope as a believer, always be ready to explain it. But do this in a gentle and respectful way... 1 Peter 3:15-16 NLT

Throughout life's journey, we will also come across many other people who are mentally blocked from coming to Christ by preconceived unbiblical ideas and false teachings about God, Satan and mankind which have already been instilled in their thinking. These people are much more difficult to convince if we do not have a good foundational knowledge of

God's Word and His character to be able to refute any false teaching they have received.

If we are trying to reach these people, we will not be effective in witnessing to them unless we know the heart of God and the content of the Bible well enough to present to them a far different concept of God than that of the warped pseudo-Christian organizations and false religions whose teachings have been leading them astray. That is why, God also tells us to:

> Study to shew thyself approved unto God, a workman
> that needeth not to be ashamed, rightly dividing the word
> of truth. 2 Timothy 2:15 KJV

The unfortunate reality is that it is extremely difficult for professing Christians who know very little of their own Bible to effectively witness to backsliders, cult members, or unbelievers who don't really know God's heart, yet they do know the Bible well enough to be able to pick and choose which verses they want to use and twist to support their own sinful lifestyles and warped concepts of God.

The book you are now reading was written to help those who do not yet follow Jesus Christ, but are curious to learn about God. However, it was also compiled with my deepest desire to assist professing Christians who want to grow in the knowledge of God so that no matter who we are witnessing to, we will not be ashamed of our lack of knowledge of God's Word. Rather, God wants us to be ready and able to explain it to anyone we come in contact with, because the Word of God does not change according to different audiences. It is exactly the same to all.

The Word of God does not change to favor anyone. It does not matter if people have a background in atheism, evolution, cults, eastern religions, or are backslidden professing Christians in danger of following Satan right into hell for their refusal to depart from a continuing sinful lifestyle. It does not make any difference if the hearer of our teaching is a total stranger or a close family member, because ALL must take the same path of personally coming to Christ to be saved and there is no other name under heaven whereby anyone on Earth can be saved.

The truth is that God is the source of our light, love and life. He is the Creator, the Savior, and the life-giver. This book will help you understand "WHY" God wants us to repent and come back to Him. Our Father God in Heaven wants us all to come to the knowledge that Satan (the destroyer and condemner of mankind to eternal damnation and domination in hell) is our real enemy, and continuing to follow the Devil today is what is ruining people's lives all over the world.

I invite you now to come with me through God's Word as we examine the Bible's revelation of the relationship between God, Satan, and the human race, and the dynamics of how God and Satan actually function in our universe. I hope that you continue with me until you firmly understand and believe that it is not God who killed Adam and Eve. It is not God who killed the people in the worldwide flood of Noah's day. It was not God who destroyed Sodom and Gomorrah.

It is also not God who murdered millions of Jews in the Holocaust. It is not God who is responsible for all of the suffering going on around the world today. Neither will it be God who will cause the deaths of billions of people during the coming Tribulation. My prayer for every reader is that by the end of this book, you will all have a better understanding that it is Satan, not God, who is our real enemy and the destroyer of the human race.

Jesus is returning soon, dear friends, and I pray that this book will open your eyes to the true character and heart of God so that you will have hope for the future and be grateful that God has not appointed us to the wrath that will be coming upon the Earth during the Great Tribulation.

If we love Him and are preparing for His coming, Father God knows that we are Christ's Bride, and what kind of loving Father, or loving Bridegroom would appoint Christ's beloved to endure seven years of the wrath of God. Our Lord does not want that for any of us. Father God wants every single one of us to be caught up to Heaven with Jesus Christ when Jesus arrives to receive His Bride.

Regardless of what you have heard out of the mouths of well-meaning, but misguided preachers, the seven year tribulation is not being sent by God as a test of the faith of the righteous. It will be permitted as a judgement and warning to the wicked who refuse to depart from their iniquities. It will not be God who is bringing all manner of destruction and death, and trying to exterminate all of mankind during the coming seven year tribulation.

The goal of the wrath of God is not to "refine" and test the righteous. It is to bring the wicked to repentance. The whole purpose of the Tribulation is to diminish God's presence on Earth for a while in order to teach humanity that we cannot survive without God. It is to convict and convince people during the tribulation that mankind must repent and come back to our loving Father in Heaven if we want to survive, because Satan is out to get the human race.

Yes, through the ministry of the two witnesses, the 144,000 and the tribulation saints who are converted and accept Christ, throughout this seven year Tribulation, Father God will continue to call the remainder of mankind to repentance and faith in Jesus, right up to the very day of Christ's arrival to set up His eternal kingdom on Earth as it is in Heaven. Then, when their blindness is finally taken away, the nation of Israel will also come to the truth that Jesus Christ is the Messiah they have been waiting for, and (as God has said), a nation shall be saved in a day.

Sadly, billions of people will die during the Tribulation, but once you more clearly understand the Scriptures and the heart of God, I hope to be able to teach you that it not be God who kills all of these people. It will be someone else who will be causing all of the death and destruction for the entire seven year Tribulation period. Satan is the guilty one. Although it is also called the wrath of God, it will actually be Satan who will be venting his wrath and his rage against humanity during the last seven years of his dominion over man in a desperately evil attempt to take as many as possible with Him when he is cast out at the end of it all.

Yet, Satan will not be successful in destroying all of mankind. Many will be saved and give their lives for Christ during the Tribulation, and Father God will place His protection around a small remnant of believers so that there will still be a tiny elect portion of humanity left to repopulate the world when Jesus returns to set up His eternal kingdom.

Yes, it will be God Himself, God the Word, God with us, the King of Kings and Lord of Lords, the Everlasting Father who will return to planet Earth in the form of Jesus Christ for the purpose of preventing all human flesh on Earth from being destroyed as a result of Satan's rule and the Antichrist's Satanically-inspired methodical self-annihilation of the human race.

So listen, beloved of God. Listen to what the Spirit of God is saying, because it is not only to the churches, but to all of humanity in these end times. God did not kill Adam and Eve and He will not be the one destroying the world in these last days either.

God is the giver of life, not the taker. He is the Creator, not the Destroyer. He is the Savior, not the Condemner. He is the source of Comfort and hope, not despair and fear. Therefore, I hope that this book will help every reader understand that God loves us with a deeply unfathomable love, but now is the time for repentance and living for Jesus Christ, because there are dark days ahead for this wicked and adulterous end times generation who want nothing to do with God, His righteousness, or His Word, and it will be Satan's wrath at the head of it all. As for Jesus, He declares in John 8:12 "I am the LIGHT of the world." Come with me now into the Word of God to explore and learn a little of what Jesus means by that statement.

CHAPTER 2

There Are Three Heavens!

OUR FATHER WHICH ART IN THE THIRD HEAVEN

Let's start on this journey of learning about God by seeing what the Bible has to say about Heaven. Anyone who knows even a little bit about the Bible will be able to tell you that when Jesus Christ's disciples asked Him to teach them how to pray, Jesus responded by telling them to say "Our Father which art in Heaven." This is the beginning phrase of what is now commonly called the Lord's Prayer, and it is followed by "Thy kingdom come on Earth as it is in Heaven."

> After this manner therefore pray ye: Our Father which art in heaven, Hallowed be thy name. Thy kingdom come, Thy will be done in earth, as it is in heaven. Matthew 6:9-10 KJV

From this small passage of the Scripture, we can learn four basic, but important Bible truths:

1. Heaven is a real place
2. Father God has a Kingdom
3. Father God's Kingdom is presently in Heaven
4. God's Kingdom and His will shall eventually come to pass on Earth as it now exists in Heaven

A great place for us to begin when teaching about the Bible is to start where everything originated "in the beginning". Even though we cannot see Heaven with our mortal eyes, God declares to us in His Word that Heaven exists. It is a very real place. Other Scriptures throughout the Bible refer to Heaven as Father God's "House" or dwelling place. Just before His death, Jesus said:

> Don't let this throw you. You trust God, don't you? Trust me. There is plenty of room for you in my Father's home. If that weren't so, would I have told you that I'm on my way to get a room ready for you? And if I'm on my way to get your room ready, I'll come back and get you so you can live where I live. And you already know the road I'm taking." John 14:1-4 MSG

In the Epistles of Paul, one of the things that the Apostle Paul reveals to us is that there are actually three heavens, and the Third Heaven is the one where God presently resides. Speaking of the Apostle John's experience which inspired him to write the Book of Revelation, Paul says:

> I know a man in Christ who fourteen years ago— whether in the body I do not know, or whether out of the body I do not know, God knows—such a one was caught up to the third heaven. And I know such a man— whether in the body or out of the body I do not know, God knows— how he was caught up into Paradise and heard inexpressible words, which it is not lawful for a man to utter. 2 Corinthians 12:2-4 NKJV

From here we can go to the Apostle John describing the experience in his own words:

> After this I looked, and, behold, a door was opened in heaven: and the first voice which I heard was as it were of a trumpet talking with me; which said, Come up hither, and I will shew thee things which must be hereafter. And immediately I was in the spirit: and, behold, a throne

was set in heaven, and one sat on the throne. Revelation
4:1-2 KJV

Here John paints us a very clear mental picture of being caught UP
to the Third Heaven and seeing God sitting on His throne. Then a short
time later John also describes seeing a huge number of angels and animals
and elders around the throne of God, literally a hundred million and
millions more. Yes, Heaven is already inhabited with billions of creatures
and beings, dear friends. When we finally go to Heaven, we are certainly
not the only ones who are going to be there:

> Then I looked, and I heard the voice of many angels
> around the throne, the living creatures, and the elders; and
> the number of them was ten thousand times ten thousand,
> and thousands of thousands. Revelation 5:11 NKJV

GOD'S CITY WILL COME DOWN FROM HEAVEN

At the end of John's Revelation, he tells of a future time when there
will be a specific city (Heavenly Jerusalem) which will come down from the
Third Heaven, and listen to this. The dimensions of this city give us a small
taste of just how large God's dwelling place really is. It also gives us a hint
that the new Earth which God will create for the Heavenly Jerusalem to
land on may be far larger than the planet Earth we now know and live on:

> Then I saw a new heaven and a new earth, for the
> old heaven and the old earth had disappeared. And the
> sea was also gone. And I saw the holy city, the New
> Jerusalem, coming down from God out of heaven like a
> bride beautifully dressed for her husband. I heard a loud
> shout from the throne, saying, "Look, God's home is now
> among his people! He will live with them, and they will
> be his people. God himself will be with them…The angel
> who talked to me held in his hand a gold measuring
> stick to measure the city, its gates, and its wall. When he
> measured it, he found it was a square, as wide as it was

long. In fact, its length and width and height were each
1,400 miles. Revelation 21:1-16 NLT

Just to put the size of this city in perspective, The United States
(including Alaska and Hawaii) covers an area of about 2680 miles long by
1582 miles wide. Furthermore, the entire area of all the dry land on Earth
equals a little over 57 million square miles.

Now try to imagine a single city that is more than half the size of the
United States on its ground floor, and then that city is also at least 1400
miles high with who knows how many levels. (Note: the KJV translates
the dimensions as 12,000 furlongs in each direction, which is about 1500
miles long by 1500 miles wide by 1500 miles high)

Some suggest that the city will be pyramidal and others believe it will
be cube-shaped, but regardless of the shape, if we very conservatively guess
that each level of the city is a mile high, the ground floor will cover almost
2 million square miles with 1399 levels above the ground floor, giving this
one city a total living space of many, many times greater than all of the dry
land currently in existence on Earth.

Yes, even though we can't see it with our mortal eyes yet, this is how
big just one city from the Third Heaven is, and the Book of Revelation
tells us that in the new Heaven and Earth there will be many nations
(suggesting many other cities) whose inhabitants will regularly travel from
their nation to visit Heavenly Jerusalem.

> And the nations of them which are saved shall walk
> in the light of it: and the kings of the earth do bring their
> glory and honour into it. And the gates of it shall not be
> shut at all by day: for there shall be no night there. And
> they shall bring the glory and honour of the nations into
> it. Revelation 21:24-26 KJV

So, when we take time to think about it a little bit, it is almost beyond
imagination to try to conceive how big the new Heaven and Earth are
going to be. Truly, God's promises are all beyond wonderful.

WHO LIVES IN THE THIRD HEAVEN?

God's Word tells us that the Third Heaven is presently the abode of Father God, the Holy Ghost (keeping in mind that the Holy Ghost also dwells within living believers), Jesus Christ, and two thirds of the angels.

Furthermore, ever since Christ rose from the dead and took the spirits of deceased believers with Him to His Father's house, Heaven has also been the dwelling place of the spirits of every deceased true believer who has ever lived on planet Earth right up to the present day. They do not have their resurrected bodies yet, but their conscious souls and spirits are now residing in Heaven, awaiting the day of the resurrection of their former bodies, which (on the day of the Rapture) will be instantly transformed into incorruptible, immortal eternal spiritual bodies.

What about God? Well, God Himself (the Father, the Word and the Holy Spirit) is from everlasting to everlasting. God is without beginning or end. He has always existed and will continue to exist forever because God is not bound by time or space. However, the Bible tells us that all the other beings in Heaven had a beginning, a time of creation, and things in Heaven were not always as they are now.

There was a point in time preceding God's creation of the material universe when God first created an innumerable quantity of angelic beings. The incredible thing about the creation of the angels is that, in spite of their great majesty and power, these angels were not ordained and destined to be God's greatest creation.

I know it is hard to believe this when you look at humanity in our present pathetically corrupted and fallen state, but God tells us that He actually created the angels to minister to those who will be the heirs of salvation and rulers of all creation. The Word of God declares that mankind (we who are God's children) will be the beings who will eventually rule the entire universe (including the angels) as co-heirs and co-rulers with Jesus Christ:

> Therefore, angels are only servants—spirits sent to care
> for people who will inherit salvation. Hebrews 1:14 NLT

Isn't that a fantastic promise? When we look further into the Word of God, we find that God created the angels to be eternal beings. They never die, but (like us) they are certainly not robots with no free will. Just like human beings, angels were also created with the freedom to choose to continue to know only God's goodness forever, or to embrace the knowledge of evil.

The Bible does not expound on exactly when or how one third of the angels exercised their freedom to reject God's will and choose to embrace evil, but we do know that often events occurring on Earth are shadowy examples of things which have occurred or will occur in heaven. Perhaps there was also a tree of knowledge of good and evil in Heaven.

We can't know for sure, because the Bible does not go into detail about the exact circumstances of the fall of the angels. What we do know from the Word of God, however, is that (at some point) Lucifer, the leader of the angels chose to disobey God, embrace evil and then he convinced one-third of the angels in heaven to follow his lead and do the same.

Then, as evil gradually poisoned their thinking, Lucifer and his followers began to hate God and hate that their purpose for existence was going to be to minister to humanity. In fact, God tells us that all of the angels who chose to embrace evil eventually became so obsessed and totally consumed with evil that there is no longer any good left in them.

Lucifer then led an angelic rebellion against God, with the foolish goal of trying to overthrow God and take over ruler ship of Heaven in order to change Heaven into a kingdom of darkness and evil:

> How art thou fallen from heaven, O Lucifer, son of the morning! How art thou cut down to the ground, which didst weaken the nations! For thou hast said in thine heart, I will ascend into heaven, I will exalt my throne above the stars of God: I will sit also upon the mount of the congregation, in the sides of the north: I will ascend above the heights of the clouds; I will be like the most High. Yet thou shalt be brought down to hell, to the sides of the pit. Isaiah 14:12-15 KJV

Needless to say, their rebellion failed. Lucifer and all of the angels who followed him were cast out of the Third Heaven, and ever since then have had to make their dwelling place and headquarters in the Second Heaven.

Satan and his evil angels still have to report all of their activities to God in the Third Heaven, as do all of the angels, but the evil angels no longer reside there, and of course, God still retains the ultimate authority over what all angels (good and evil) can and cannot do.

Actually, there is much evidence in Scripture that by the time God created the Earth, Lucifer and his followers had already been evicted from the Third Heaven and taken up residence in the Second Heaven, because in the Scriptures, God declares to us that:

> For You are not a God who takes pleasure in wickedness. Nor shall evil dwell with You. Psalm 5:4 NKJV

Evidently, it was at the time of Lucifer's expulsion from the Third Heaven that God revoked Lucifer's original name and renamed this evil angel. God took away his original name "Lucifer" (meaning "light-bearer", "extreme brightness-like a star that can be seen even in the morning) and gave him the names "Satan" (adversary-accuser) and "Devil" (devastator). God also identifies Satan throughout Scripture as the serpent, the dragon, the one who has the power of death, and the "father" of all lies and liars.

WHERE IS SATAN'S PRESENT REALM?

There are actually quite a few clues throughout the Bible regarding the location of Satan's present dwelling place (the Second Heaven), but one of the most important ones is given to us by the Apostle John:

> This is the message which we have heard from Him and declare to you, that God is light and in Him is no darkness at all. 1 John 1:5 NKJV

This is actually one of the key Scriptures in the Word of God to help us understand what is going on in the unseen spiritual realm around us.

All we have to do is look up to the sky and logically follow the information that God has given us.

We have just read that God is light and in Him is no darkness at all, and God will not allow darkness (evil) to dwell with Him. Therefore, the logical conclusion is that there is no darkness at all in the Third Heaven.

We also know from Revelation that when God creates the new heavens and earth that there will not be any darkness there either. God's Glory will actually fill the entirety of the new Heaven and Earth and emanate from within every human inhabitant who dwells there:

> There shall be no night there: They need no lamp nor light of the sun, for the Lord God gives them light. And they shall reign forever and ever. Revelation 22:5 NKJV

The Apostle Paul also gives us a clue to the location of the 2nd Heaven (Satan's present domain) in the Book of Ephesians:

> Put on the whole armor of God that you may be able to stand against the wiles of the devil. For we do not wrestle against flesh and blood, but against principalities, against powers, against the rulers of the darkness of this age, against spiritual hosts of wickedness in the heavenly places. Ephesians 6:11-12 NKJV

So, think about it for a moment. If God is light, and in him is no darkness at all, where is the darkest, most deadly heavenly place that you can think of? That's right. The darkest, most toxic, most deadly place in existence is the vast expanse in which our material universe exists. The place which we now call "outer space" is actually the "Second Heaven", the present realm or domain of Satan.

Satan is the ruler of the darkness in which the Earth, moon, planets, sun and stars presently exist. From God's own descriptions, I am inclined to believe that this Second Heaven that we now know as outer space was not always a deadly wasteland of darkness and toxicity to all biological life. Certainly, God would not have created it that way.

No, I believe that when Satan was ousted from the Third Heaven, he put all of his effort into transforming the Second Heaven into its present toxic state of darkness and death, with the goal of trying to prevent God from succeeding with His plan to create mankind and have us rule over him.

Satan knows that the Word of God promises one day mankind will rule with Jesus Christ over all of creation INCLUDING THE ANGELS. The Devil hates that promise, and from the very beginning, he has been doing everything he can to stop the Word of God from becoming a reality.

However, I tell you that no being in the universe, not human or angel can ever outthink, out plan or outmaneuver God. Let's now open our Bibles and take a look now at how easily God defeated Satan's plan to stop the human race from coming into existence. In fact, the Scriptures reveal that God created our home (the Earth) right smack dab in the middle of Satan's dark and deadly domain, and Satan had no authority or power to prevent it from happening. There was nothing the Devil could do to stop God from creating the Earth, protecting it from all evil, and giving mankind dominion over it.

IN THE BEGINNING GOD CREATED

Let's review what we have already talked about. What was it that God created in the beginning? He created the Three Heavens and the Earth.

In the beginning God created the heavens and the earth. Genesis 1:1 KJV

In the beginning God created the Third Heaven as the original dwelling place for Himself and the angels. God also created the Second Heaven. This was the vast expanse of outer space where God decreed that this present universe would be created and exist.

Then Lucifer and a third of the angels embraced evil and their natures degenerated until they became totally evil. They were all evicted from the Third Heaven after Satan led a failed attempt to try to depose God and take over the Third Heaven.

Then Satan and his evil angelic followers went to work transforming the Second Heaven into a desolate realm of deadly darkness in an effort to thwart God's creation of mankind. I'll talk a little more about that in a minute, but first, let's take a look at what the Bible has to say about the First Heaven and its purpose.

Actually, the First Heaven is what is keeping all life on Earth from being instantly destroyed by Satan. The First Heaven is God's hedge of protection around planet Earth which includes the life-giving atmosphere surrounding our planet. It is the First Heaven which protects us from being burned to a crisp by the sun, poisoned by cosmic radiation, choked to death by lack of oxygen, or instantly frozen into a Popsicle by the -454 degree F temperature of outer space.

It is the creation of the First Heaven which enabled there to be liquid water on Earth, even before God created the Sun, and yes, I did say that God created the Earth before He created the sun, moon and stars, regardless of what you have been previously taught in your church or in our godless schools, universities and science academies.

I know that many people reading this book have already had years of Evolutionist propaganda influencing your thinking, but if you bear with me for a few chapters, I will show you from the Word of God how none of what they have taught you is true, and they have been deceiving people.

> The earth was without form, and void; and darkness *was on the face of the deep. And the Spirit of God was hovering over the face of the waters.* Then God said, "Let there be light"; and there was light. And God saw the light that *it was good; and God divided the light from the darkness. God called the light Day, and the darkness He called Night. So the evening and the morning were the first day.* Genesis 1:2-5 NKJV

Let's take a closer look at God's creation of the Earth. The Bible tells us that the Earth started out formless, void (of life) and completely covered in water, with the Holy Spirit hovering over the water to keep the water in liquid form and protected from Satan's deadly domain.

The Bible says that when the Earth was first created, it was created in the midst Satan's realm of total darkness. As for those who think that this must be talking about a "re-creation" on top of billions of years of evolutionary violent destruction and death because God would not create the Earth "without form and void", we'll talk a bit about that skewed perspective in the chapters to come. For now, I pray that you will be patient and continue to follow along in God's Word as we look deeper into the whole matter of the creation of Earth and the rest of the universe.

CHAPTER 3

Faith in Evolution vs Faith in God

EVOLUTION IS A RELIGION, NOT A SCIENCE

I know that some of you are grinding your teeth right now because (for your whole lives) you have been taught that the philosophies of Evolution are proven science, but you have believed a lie. None of the outrageous claims of Evolutionists have ever been proven scientifically. In fact, as mankind becomes more knowledgeable and we continue to advance in science, the concepts of evolution are becoming more scientifically improbable every year.

Contrary to the claims of Evolutionists, from a scientific perspective, it is somewhat illogical that Atheists and Evolutionists mock the idea of the universe having a Creator and intelligent design, yet have no problem believing and teaching that the universe just popped into being from nothing. It takes a huge amount of unsupported faith to believe in that the universe came from nothing. Essentially your faith is in nothing, and is based on nothing, which you believe spawned everything. It is not really a very logical or scientific way of thinking.

Think about it. Evolutionists refuse to believe that life on Earth has a Creator, but they have no trouble believing that life randomly (without design or purpose) just suddenly appeared on Earth and then just as mysteriously and magically, single celled organisms developed the incredibly complex ability to reproduce themselves and evolve into higher forms.

Where is evidence of evolution from one kind of life form to another? There is none! However, in spite of the fact that there is no scientific evidence in over 6000 years of recorded history of any single life form naturally evolving into a different kind of life form, Evolutionists today still doggedly adhere to the claim that it did happen, using the argument that it took billions of years to occur. That is not science. That is faith. Belief in Evolution is not science. It is religion, and it is FALSE religion.

Nonetheless, in our modern advanced society, today's educators, scientists, politicians and even some spiritual leaders (the self-proclaimed apex of evolutionary intellectual development) still religiously continue to spread and endorse their claims of evolution based on nothing more than faith alone without any real scientific evidence to back up their claims.

The incredible irony of all this only increases when we observe that many of these same scientists are dedicated to their goals of "creating life" themselves. They clone animals. They grow living tissue in labs. They want to use long dead DNA to bring extinct species back to life. They want to be Creators. They have dreams of becoming little gods, yet they refuse to acknowledge that there is a God in Heaven who is already the one Creator and Father of the entire existing universe.

THE ARTISTRY AND SCIENCE OF GOD

Evolutionists have long argued that faith in God is nothing more than ignorant superstition. Yet those who take time to really study the Bible will find that it speaks of God as being the epitome of intelligent artistic design and unlimited scientific creativeness.

The first scientific law of thermodynamics (also called the law of conservation of energy) states that neither matter nor energy can be created or destroyed. However, under the right circumstances, energy can be changed to matter and matter to energy. Renowned hero of science Albert Einstein was on the right track when he came up with $E=mc^2$ (energy equals mass times the speed of light squared), the theory being that if mass travels fast enough, it converts into energy, and if energy is slowed, it can be converted into matter.

Do you remember reading earlier in 1 John 1:2 where the Bible reveals to us that God is LIGHT? Light is a form of energy, and the Bible also tells us that God has no beginning or end. He has always existed. God is an unlimited source of Spiritual energy and He manifests himself in LIGHT. Although science has recently learned that dark matter and dark energy also exists (Satan and his angels), the Bible declares that there is no darkness at all in God. God IS Light.

Are you beginning to see how it is scientifically feasible that God, an eternal being of unlimited spiritual energy could have the capability of transforming some of His personal light energy into matter in order to "create" and mold the Earth we live on, and make it into a form that pleases Him?

Let's go back to the book of Genesis now and I will try to help paint a mental picture for you of how the Earth and the universe really came into being. We start with God choosing a spot right in the middle of Satan's totally dark and deadly domain of outer space (the Second Heaven) and God converting some of His energy into matter to create the Earth.

Our planet started out completely immersed in water with the Spirit of God hovering over the waters using His energy to contain everything, warm it and protect it from the ravages of Satan's dark and destructive domain of outer space.

> Then God said, "Let there be light"; and there was light. And God saw the light that it *was good; and God divided the light from the darkness.* God called the light Day, and the darkness He called Night. So the evening and the morning were the first day. Genesis 1: 3-5 NKJV

What we learn from this Scripture is that the first light to shine on planet Earth did not even come from the sun because the sun is not actually older than the Earth, as the Evolutionists teach. When the Earth was first created, the first light which shone upon it came directly from God Himself, because the sun, moon and stars had not been created yet.

One thing that is often missed here by those who only know the English Scriptures is that the Hebrew word translated here as "night" actually means "twisting or turning away from the light." This indicates here that God is talking about starting our planet rotating on its axis.

This by itself reveals to us that the "first day" being described here is indeed a literal twenty-four hour day. It is a turning away from God toward the darkness, a rotation on an invisible axis, not some extended trillion year "gap" of time as some people are mistakenly teaching in certain Christian churches today.

THERE IS NO GAP BETWEEN GENESIS 1:1 & 1:2

While we are on the subject of creation, I believe it is important to go back and talk a little more about Genesis

> In the beginning God created the heavens and the earth. The earth was without form, and void; and darkness *was on the face of the deep. And the Spirit of God was hovering over the face of the waters.* Genesis 1:1-2 KJV

Unfortunately, there are some Christians in our generation who have been so browbeaten and indoctrinated into the false belief that evolution is true that they have tried to marry evolution to Christianity by promoting the unbiblical teaching in the past couple of centuries that there is a "gap" of billions or trillions of years between Genesis 1:1 and Genesis 1:2.

Their logic for doing this stems from their supposition that God would not create the Earth to be formless and void. They reason that the Hebrew phrase translated as "the earth *was* without form and void" should be translated as "the Earth *became* without form and void" just because the same Hebrew word is sometimes used elsewhere in the Bible to say "*became*".

However, there is nothing in the context of Genesis to suggest that this should be done. The only reason that they want to change the Word of God here is so that the change fits their mistaken presupposition that evolution is true.

Through this changing of the Word of God, they come to the unbiblical conclusion that there was life on Earth for billions of years previous to the creation of Adam and Eve in order to reconcile the Evolutionists claims of the existence of dinosaurs, prehistoric man and billions of years of life, death and destruction before the creation of Adam and Eve. Then they suggest that the Earth BECAME without form and void as a result of an "extinction level event" and remained lifeless and void until God recreated it later on, followed by the creation of Adam and Eve and all other life on Earth as we now know it.

This kind of unscriptural teaching opens up a whole can of worms Biblically. The absolute worst way to try to understand the Bible is to start with a preconceived notion and then take Bible passages out of context and try to twist them to make them support non-biblical ideas and teachings.

In the case of this "gap" theory, you would have to re-write large portions of Scripture to make them agree with some people's attempts to try to conform the Bible to evolution. There is only enough time and space to touch on a few of the contradictions here, but hopefully, it will be enough to prove my point.

1. Evolution presumes that the sun must be older than the Earth because there could not have been warmth and light on Earth without the sun, but Genesis 1:2-10 tells us that this is a lie because God created light to shine on the Earth on the first day of creation.
2. Evolution teaches that the sun, moon, and stars are older than the Earth, but Genesis 1:14-19 tells us that the Earth was created first and the sun, moon and stars were not created until later, on the fourth day, and they were created for MAN'S benefit.
3. Evolutionists teach that water in liquid form could not exist on Earth without their god, the sun. Genesis 1:1-11 tells us that this is a lie because the sun was not created until the fourth day, yet there was moving water on the first day.
4. Evolution dictates that plant life could not possibly exist and live on Earth without the sun, but the same passage again exposes this as a lie because God created plant life on the third day and did not create the sun until the fourth day.
5. Evolution wrongly presupposes that there were billions of years of death and destruction on Earth before the creative account of Genesis, but the Word of God declares that in the beginning, the

Earth and everything that God created on it was VERY GOOD before any life was created.

6. In the beginning, if microscopic life was the first form of life, amoebic unevolved life forms would have had no cognition of evil or propensity to sin, so why would they die? No, dear friends. The Bible tells us that in the beginning there was no death, and death did not appear and begin to corrupt creation until later on when Adam embraced evil. (Genesis 3). Death came by man (1 Cor. 15:21)

7. Evolution states that the dinosaurs died out millions and billions of years ago, but the Word of God declares in one of the oldest books of the Bible, the book of Job that the largest land creature ever created, the "behemoth" had bones like beams and had a tail like a mighty cedar tree, yet the creature was created at the same time as man.

Did dinosaurs actually live at the same time as Adam and Eve, some surviving until after the flood before becoming extinct? When you read the following Scripture, let me tell you that we can deduce (from the record of Job's extended lifespan) that Job and his contemporaries likely lived at a time not very long after the flood of Noah's day, probably just a generation or two before Abraham.

This was a historical time when man and animals still had much longer lifespans than they do today and the dinosaurs had not become totally extinct yet. Noah lived for another 349 years after he exited the Ark (for a total of 950 years), and Genesis 11 tells us that Noah's son Shem was 98 years old when he exited the Ark, had a son when he was 100 and lived for another 500 years after that.)

How could there have been dinosaurs on the Ark? Well, there is nothing in the Bible which says that all or any of the animals had to be full grown when they entered the Ark, only that they were male and female. Therefore, the real question we should be asking ourselves is whether or not baby or juvenile dinosaurs could have been on the Ark, and then exited with Noah and continued to live and grow for many centuries until they reached full size, and that, of course is a very real possibility.

One thing that we do know from scientific excavation of fossils is that even the largest of dinosaurs all started out comparatively small, hatching from eggs not much larger than footballs. The scientific key to their great size lies in how long they lived, not how big they started out.

Another thing we know from science is that there is an important difference between reptiles and mammals. Like trees in the forest, many reptiles continue to grow every year of their lives. Within their species, the biggest crocodiles are the oldest ones. The biggest snakes are the oldest ones.

Just imagine how big some reptiles could get if they lived for over 900 years, as man did in the beginning. In fact, we don't even need to imagine. God tells us how big they got. Even in Job's generation, there were still a few of these gigantic creatures remaining, and God used them as an example when confronting Job. Let's take a look at what God says to us in the book of Job:

> Behold now behemoth, which I made with thee; he eateth grass as an ox. Lo now, his strength is in his loins, and his force is in the navel of his belly. He moveth his tail like a cedar: the sinews of his stones are wrapped together. His bones are as strong pieces of brass; his bones are like bars of iron. He is the chief of the ways of God: he that made him can make his sword to approach unto him. Job 40:15-19 KJV

Now listen to me CAREFULLY. If you have a Bible version which falsely identifies this animal as a hippo, rhino, elephant or any other modern animal, they are wrong. This is not the animal being described here as the one who was created at the same time as Job and the "chief" or largest of all animals. All of the largest land animals on Earth today have tails like whisk brooms.

The only animals in existence that we know of who had tails like mighty cedar trees were dinosaurs known as titanosaurs, weighing as much as 12 elephants and having bodies over 100 feet long. Yes, they were the largest of dinosaurs AND most had tails like mighty cedar trees.

According to the book of Job, they were roaming the Earth when Adam and Eve were created, and there were still a few of them around in Job's day. The extinction of the dinosaurs came about during and after the flood, not before it.

We'll talk more about the false claims of evolution later on. For now, I hope that this is enough to make at least one point, and we can move on from here to talk about how the creation of our planet and the rest of the universe actually occurred, according to God's Word.

GOD HAS THE HEART OF AN ARTIST

Listen to the Spirit of God, dear friends. Don't listen to vain evolutionary fantasies. The reason that the Earth started out without form and void is that our Father in Heaven is a gifted Artist, not a wizard or magician. God did not just pop the world into existence in its finished state. God wanted to get His hands dirty, molding and making the Earth into something beautiful, the same way He did with the pile of dirt and water that became Adam and the way God used the living tissue and DNA from Adam's rib to create Eve:

> And yet, O Lord, you are our Father. We are the clay,
> and you are the potter. We all are formed by your hand.
> Isaiah 64:8 NLT

Now, let's take another look at God's creation of the Earth and study it from an artist's standpoint. In Genesis 1, we see God beginning the creation of our planet by converting His Spiritual energy into the elemental basics of matter in solid, liquid, and gaseous form.

Essentially, on the first day of creation, God went into the middle of the Second Heaven (Satan's dark realm) and created a ball of rock and dirt surrounded by water, which the Holy Spirit hovered over, enveloping it to keep the water in liquid form. Lovingly, God warmed, contained and protected the Earth from Satan's deadly environment.

Then God generated light directly from Himself to shine on the Earth and started rotating the Earth on its axis with the rotation from light to darkness and back to light forming the first 24 hour day. God's next step was to mold the "First Heaven", a gaseous atmosphere over Earth which would be capable of protecting our planet against the deadly ravages of outer space.

Then God said, "Let there be a space between the waters, to separate the waters of the heavens from the waters of the earth." And that is what happened. God made this space to separate the waters of the earth from the waters of the heavens. God called the space "sky." And evening passed and morning came, marking the second day. Genesis 1:6-8 NLT

Now, once again, listen carefully. This is a very important Scripture for several reasons. First, it is a vivid description of God's creation of Earth's original atmosphere. Second it is God's written record to us that our planet's original atmosphere was decidedly different from the one we know today. Thirdly, it gives us a starting point for a better understanding of how the Biblical account of the worldwide flood is actually a very feasible scientific possibility.

What God is telling us here is that during the formation of Earth, on the second day of creation, God moved a huge amount of water from the surface of the Earth to a place where the balance between gravity and the centrifugal force of the Earth's rotation would hold this water in Earth's upper atmosphere as an outer protective canopy of water totally surrounding the entire planet.

We shall see later how that this protective layer of water in the Earth's upper atmosphere played a vital role in many aspects of the existence of life on Earth during the first 1600 plus years of creation before the global flood of Noah's day, affecting the longevity of men and beasts.

> Then God said, "Let the waters beneath the sky flow together into one place, so dry ground may appear." And that is what happened. God called the dry ground "land" and the waters "seas." And God saw that it was good. Genesis 1: 9-10 NLT

Here we have a description of God opening channels into a worldwide subterranean aquifer which was designed to serve as a buffer zone for the purpose of separating and protecting the Earth's outer crust from the Earth's inner crust and the molten magma beneath it.

Just as the canopy in the upper Earth's atmosphere protected our planet from cosmic radiation and excesses of heat and cold from space, so also did the subterranean waters act as a safety buffer between the Earth's outer crust and the inner crust of the planet which holds the molten magma of the Earth's core safely contained. As God opened up the ground and the surface water on Earth receded into the subterranean aquifer beneath the planet's surface, dry ground (not massive mountains) appeared. God called the dry ground "land" and the waters, He called "seas".

Let's create another mental picture now of what the original Earth looked like as God created it. Here we have the original Earth with low mountains and gentle valleys, and everything would have been easily traversable by man and beast alike. The protruding land mass was interspersed with relatively shallow seas with much of the water on the planet being suspended in the upper atmosphere and submerged within the world wide subterranean aquifer.

> Then God said, "Let the land sprout with vegetation— every sort of seed-bearing plant, and trees that grow seed-bearing fruit. These seeds will then produce the kinds of plants and trees from which they came." And that is what happened. The land produced vegetation—all sorts of seed-bearing plants, and trees with seed-bearing fruit. Their seeds produced plants and trees of the same kind. And God saw that it was good. And evening passed and morning came, marking the third day. Genesis 1:11-13 NLT

So, the scenario up to this point in time is that the Earth and its atmosphere have been created. The Earth is being warmed and illuminated by light radiating directly from God Himself. The planet is being protected from Satan's domain by a massive water canopy suspended in the Earth's upper atmosphere. Earth is also being protected from its own molten core by a worldwide aquifer that God has inserted between the Earth's inner and outer crust.

We are now at the place in Earth's history where God declares that He then created all vegetation. Take note that this occurs on the third day of creation. The sun, moon and stars have not even been created yet, but God is providing light and heat and atmosphere. He is creating and sustaining plant life on Earth solely through the power of His own Spiritual energy.

Now, just in case some people are shaking their heads and saying that this is ridiculous, I want you to think about the space station currently orbiting our planet. They don't really need the sun. Any type of light would power their photovoltaic panels to provide light, heat and atmosphere. Their atmosphere is also self-contained and they can grow food with artificial lighting. Criminals also grow and harvest marihuana underground using artificial light, and these plants never see sunlight until they are harvested.

Think about it. If we puny humans can accomplish this with our limited knowledge and technology, imagine what our eternal God is capable of. How vain it is of man to be so proud of our own achievements and yet so unwilling to believe that God is infinitely greater, wiser and more powerful than the sons and daughters of men.

I believe that God did exactly what He said He did. He converted some of His personal energy to matter and placed it into the middle of Satan's dark and deadly domain, warming it, lighting it and calling it heaven and Earth.

Then God molded and shaped the Earth into a form that pleased Him, a form capable of sustaining all biological life. Then God started creating life, beginning with vegetation, all before the creation of the rest of the universe. People can believe something else if they want to, but that is what God says He did in His Word, and I believe it.

CHAPTER 4

God Creates the Rest of the Universe

THE UNIVERSE WAS CREATED FOR MANKIND

Evolutionists tend to say that Christians are full of vanity and self-importance to think that the entire universe was created by God for our benefit. Yet, this is not stopping Evolutionists from trying to get out to the moon and other planets so they can claim them for their own glory. Like little gods, their goal is to create new human civilizations on the moon and other planets. However, more importantly, what does the Bible say about it all?

> Then God said, "Let lights appear in the sky to separate the day from the night. Let them be signs to mark the seasons, days, and years. Let these lights in the sky shine down on the earth." And that is what happened. God made two great lights—the larger one to govern the day, and the smaller one to govern the night. He also made the stars. God set these lights in the sky to light the earth, to govern the day and night, and to separate the light from the darkness. And God saw that it was good. And evening passed and morning came, marking the fourth day. Genesis 1: 14-19 NLT

Do you get what the Bible is saying here? God is saying that on the fourth day, He created the sun to replace the light that God Himself had been providing until that day. God also created the moon and the stars on that day, declaring that their purpose was so that even when the Earth turns away from the sun, humanity would not be subjected to the total blackness of Satan's realm. There would still be at least some light shining on our planet.

So the universe is NOT older than the sun, and the sun is NOT older than the moon. They were all created at the same time on the same day. God also explains here that the sun, moon and stars were created as signs for the recording of time, marking days, seasons and years, an attribute that is only useful to human beings.

Evolutionists will argue that the stars are so far away that the light from them would take millions of years to reach us. Therefore, they argue that everything else in space must be much older than the Earth.

To these people, I say this. If God is able to create the whole universe in a day and create light to sustain life on Earth without any material source, I assure you that it is no problem for God to create the light coming from the stars at the same time He creates the stars so that (as Genesis has just said) all God has to do is say "Let lights appear in the sky" and they will be instantly visible from Earth. After all, I am not vain enough to suggest that God's abilities and scientific grasp are not far superior to ours. We now have the technological ability to create a space station to orbit the Earth, but when was the last time man created a solar system or a galaxy?

You see, God knows all things. God knew right from the very beginning that man would reject Him. Yet, it was still God's desire to both hinder Satan's ability to do evil, and give humanity comfort and hope for the future. God did this through eliminating the terror of being immersed in total darkness at night, and by utilizing the universe itself to help humanity measure the passage of time toward God's promise of eventual redemption from Satan's dominion.

THE UNIVERSE WAS CREATED TO GIVE US HOPE

Let me give you some examples of what I am talking about. Before the rest of the universe was created, everything was already in place to sustain life on Earth. Once God had started the Earth rotating on its axis and the planet's atmosphere and ecological system was in place, the light and heat emanating from God's presence during the day was adequate to sustain biological life on Earth.

However, there was nothing to repel the total darkness and hinder evil during the night. There was nothing to indicate the passage of time during a single day and no way to measure time beyond a single day. There was just total light as the Earth turned toward God and total darkness as it turned away again, and for man, that would have been a fearful repetition of the terror of total darkness, night after night for our entire existence.

Have you ever been in total darkness, deprived of all light, unable to discern your surroundings to move around, unable to see even your hand in front of your face? Most city people have never known what it is like to be outside at night in the country, but I grew up in the country when there were some nights that the clouds shrouded the moon and the stars, and there are no streetlights.

Even then, you were not in total darkness. There was still a little light. You could usually see a couple of feet in front of you, but it did not take very long before the sounds of the night become exaggerated and frightening, and you couldn't wait to get out of the darkness and back to your home, or at least somewhere where there was more light.

If you take a tour through the some of the more tourist-oriented caves in the world, in a few of them, they will turn all of the lights off so people can experience what it is like to be in total darkness, but they always warn people that it will only last a couple of minutes because it is a truly disturbing experience to have your eyes wide open trying to see, and you cannot even see your fingers right in front of your nose. For some, it's truly terrifying.

When people go blind, one of their biggest challenges is overcoming the "fear" of not being able to see, because Satan is the spirit of fear and the ruler of darkness. When I was younger, I can remember my dad telling me that I could go out and play, but I had to be home by dark because "nothing good happens after dark".

Yes, that is a bit of an exaggeration of course, but dad had a good point. Even today, Satan and those who follow the Devil conceal much of their wicked activities in darkness. A lot of evil in this world occurs after dark when people know (or at least think) that they cannot be seen.

Imagine how terrible it would have been for humanity to see the Earth rotating away from God's light every day and then have to endure the next twelve hours in total darkness, especially after the fall, when evil became an integral part of human nature and the world around us.

Every night would have been horrifying. So instead, God gave us the visible universe to help us gauge the passage of time of seconds and minutes and hours and days and weeks and months and years, but more importantly so that our nights would not be enveloped in total darkness and dread. God tells us that He created the moon at the same time as the sun so that the sun's light would be reflected off the moon at night and the Earth would not be in total darkness when it turns away from the sun, and He created the stars for the same reason.

The ability to tell time is also important to us. When we want a soft boiled egg, we know to cook it for three minutes. When a loved one has to go somewhere and they say they will be back in 36 hours, we know exactly when to expect them. When a woman is in the agony of childbirth, once she nears the nine month date, she has the knowledge and hope that soon her suffering will be over and she will have the reward of a son or daughter.

When we are in the middle of a winter freeze or summer heat wave, we have hope for the future because we know that in a month or so things will be back to normal, and we know all this because God gave us the celestial bodies to help us measure time.

Even now, as an older man in my sixties, I am aware that my eyes and ears are growing dull and my body hurts more and grows weaker every year. Yet, I also know that this will not last forever because every day that I live, I know I am getting closer to the day I will see Jesus, whether through death, or by being caught up to be with Him when He returns for His bride in these last days.

I don't blame God for any of the trials of life because I know the identity of the one who is responsible for human suffering. Furthermore, I know that God has set a time and a quantity limit on human suffering that Satan can inflict. I am comforted knowing that God has given us about 70 years or a little more for our present lifespan, and although some even live to over 100, eventually mortal life ends for all of us. Then we go to be with the Lord and all evil and suffering ceases, with only the goodness and blessings of God remaining for the rest of eternity.

Yes, dear friends, the universe is not older than the Earth. It was created by God for our comfort and benefit, to give us confident hope in the future. That is not human vanity. That is just having faith in God's Word. Then, as an added blessing and enjoyment, God also gave us every other kind of life on Earth. What a magnificent and artistic God He is. How wonderful it is that God loves His children so much that He created so many other marvelous life forms in order for us to enjoy their beauty and goodness, generation after generation.

GOD FILLED THE EARTH WITH LIFE.

I am so glad that we are not the only form of animal life that God created on Earth. Life would have been a far more boring existence without animals to interact with. I never cease to marvel at all of the truly magnificent creatures which surround us on every side.

During my own lifespan, I have been blessed to have numerous animals over the years as pets and they have all been wonderful and loving companions. No, man did not evolve from any other animals. God created them all for our delight and benefit. He filled the Earth with a whole myriad of fantastic creatures for us to marvel at and delight in. We are the ones who eventually messed that up by embracing evil and welcoming it into our dominion.

> Then God said, "Let the waters swarm with fish and other life. Let the skies be filled with birds of every kind." So God created great sea creatures and every living thing that scurries and swarms in the water, and every sort of bird—each producing offspring of the same kind. And God saw that it was good. Then God blessed them, saying, "Be fruitful and multiply. Let the fish fill the seas, and let the birds multiply on the earth." And evening passed and morning came, marking the fifth day. Genesis 1:20-23 NLT

Here we now have the Bible proclaiming that on the fifth day, God created all aquatic and bird life, each created with the ability to reproduce AFTER ITS OWN KIND, which is in direct contradiction to Evolutionists and the Gap Theory.

These false religions suggest that all life evolved from microscopic life forms. They contradict God's Word by saying that birds evolved from aquatic life and reptiles, in spite of the fact that there is no real scientific proof of any of this. They make their claims in spite of the fact that their fantasies are in direct denial of God's declaration that birds and fish were created at the same time, on the same day, before the creation of land animals.

> Then God said, "Let the earth produce every sort of animal, each producing offspring of the same kind— livestock, small animals that scurry along the ground, and wild animals." And that is what happened. God made all sorts of wild animals, livestock, and small animals, each able to produce offspring of the same kind. And God saw that it was good. Genesis 1:24-25 NLT

Next we have the record of God creating all land animals each able to reproduce AFTER THEIR OWN KIND, and God does this on a separate day to specifically emphasize that these are different "kinds" of animals from birds and aquatic life forms.

Furthermore, God deliberately excludes mankind from all other created animals, declaring in the very next verses that humanity is divinely unique from all other life on Earth in that we are the only life form on Earth created in God's own image and after His likeness. Then God states that man too was created with the ability to reproduce, but only after our own KIND, refuting any type of human evolution from lower life forms:

> Then God said, "Let us make human beings in our image, to be like us. They will reign over the fish in the sea, the birds in the sky, the livestock, all the wild animals on the earth, and the small animals that scurry along the ground." So God created human beings in his own image.

> In the image of God he created them; male and female
> he created them. Then God blessed them and said, "Be
> fruitful and multiply. Fill the earth and govern it. Reign
> over the fish in the sea, the birds in the sky, and all the
> animals that scurry along the ground." Genesis 1: 26-
> 28 NLT

Here we see the Scriptures explaining that at the time of the beginning of man's creation, God was ruling in the Third Heaven, Satan was ruling in the Second Heaven, and Adam was ruling in the First Heaven.

We will soon go into greater detail regarding what God means by saying we are created in His image. But here we see that man was not only created in God's own image and likeness, he was created by God to reign over, or have dominion over all other life on Earth. In other words, we were created to rule over and be God's caretakers of planet Earth and all other life upon it. My, oh my! We have certainly messed up that duty and privilege, haven't we?

We can also see from the next few verses that God had created plant life for the food and nourishment of all animal life. The Bible indicates that the whole Earth at the time of creation was vegetarian and there was no predation among any of the animals. Neither would there have been any death in the animal kingdom in the beginning.

This is another contradiction to the Gap Theory, which adheres to the Evolutionary fantasy that the higher forms of animal life evolved through "natural selection" and "survival of the fittest" (predation upon weaker species) as Darwin described it. The whole premise of evolution depends on the false presumption of billions of years of violence, destruction and death on Earth, which God's Word tells us is a lie. In the beginning, there was no death AT ALL before Adam rejected God's goodness in order to experience evil.

> Then God said, "Look! I have given you every seed-
> bearing plant throughout the earth and all the fruit trees
> for your food. And I have given every green plant as food
> for all the wild animals, the birds in the sky, and the small
> animals that scurry along the ground—everything that

has life." And that is what happened. Then God looked over all he had made, and he saw that it was very good! And evening passed and morning came, marking the sixth day. Genesis 1:29-31 NLT

We have just gone through our omnipotent God's description of the first six (literal twenty-four hour) days of creation of the entire universe. Then the Bible tells us that on the seventh day, God rested, blessed the seventh day and declared it holy, for it was the day that God rested (can you blame Him) from all that He had created.

After all of this, God then gives us a description of man's first home, a beautiful garden paradise called "Eden" and the Lord goes into a lot more detail about the creation of man and about how the Earth's ecosystem functioned before the flood. Let's start with another clue from the Bible about the world's first ecosystem as the Lord describes it in Genesis:

> This *is the history of the heavens and the earth when they were created, in the day that the Lord God made the earth and the heavens,* before any plant of the field was in the earth and before any herb of the field had grown. For the Lord God had not caused it to rain on the earth, and *there was no man to till the ground; but a mist went up from the earth and watered the whole face of the ground.* Genesis 2: 4-6 NKJV

Here we have God (through Moses) explaining to us in Genesis that at this point in human history there was no rain. He was not saying that it just hadn't rained up until the vegetation was created, as some have speculated. Moses was saying that in the pre-flood ecosystem, it did not rain at all.

Rather, because of the type of sub-tropical water-laden atmosphere that God had put in place above the Earth, every morning ample water condensed on the surface of the planet to provide (along with the four rivers flowing from Eden) all the water necessary for all plant life on Earth to thrive and animal life to drink. It was somewhat like the closed ecosystem of a terrarium or greenhouse, but on a planet wide scale, and much more efficient.

I say it was a sub-tropical climate worldwide because the water canopy completely surrounding the entire Earth would have been a marvelously effective barrier to the extremes of hot and cold which we now experience in our harsher present ecosystem. This explains why scientists have discovered sub-tropical vegetation in the digestive tracts of mammoths unearthed in the far north, as well as in the rock strata from the same areas.

The water canopy in the upper atmosphere served to diffuse the sun's heat during the day providing a more temperate climate (even at the equator) than we now have. There were no deserts at the equator, no frozen wastelands at the poles, and no life threatening temperatures anywhere on Earth. Then at night, the temperature dipped just enough to produce a heavy dew which watered the entire planet enough so that every form of plant life would flourish abundantly.

Yet, in the beginning, there was no one to cultivate and care for God's special garden (the Garden of Eden) so God created His own offspring, a man and a woman to tend His Garden. Yes, by creating man (male and female) in His own image and after His own likeness, the Bible tells us that God was bearing offspring. God was producing His own children in human form, created to be loved and cherished for eternity.

That's right. God does not need human sexuality to produce children. He didn't need it for Adam. He didn't need it for Eve, and God didn't need it for Jesus either. Then, when all of God's creation was completed, God made a specific point of declaring that everything He had created was "very good".

CHAPTER 5

Details About The Creation of Man

ADAM-THE FIRST HUMAN BEING ON EARTH

Here again we have the testimony in the Word of God that mankind is not evolved from any other form of life on Earth. The Bible specifically states that God made and molded the first man's body from the elements of the Earth itself, and then directly breathed His Spirit into that biological body which He had created, and the man became a living person, a spiritual being with emotion, intellect and will, a spiritual "child" of God functioning in the material world through a biological body:

> Then the Lord God formed the man from the dust of the ground. He breathed the breath of life into the man's nostrils, and the man became a living person. Genesis 2:7 NLT

God declares that He made man directly from the dust of the ground, but because the Atheists and the Evolutionists do not want to acknowledge God and are ungrateful to God for their own existence, they refuse to believe what God says in His Word. Instead, they have invented a fantasy, a lie, that mankind originally evolved from some mentally deficient troglodyte branch of primate that was only a little higher on the intelligence scale than a modern chimpanzee or gorilla. But are their claims really scientific? Or are they no more than the vain fantasies and unfounded beliefs of a false religion?

As far as the composition of the human body goes, the Bible is perfectly accurate. When our bodies die and our spirit and soul vacate the body, there is nothing left but matter (flesh, bone, water composed of the basic elements found anywhere on Earth). If you burn a human body or if it is left to decompose out in the elements long enough, it returns to the dirt or dust from which it came.

So, is the idea of a "creator" of life so far-fetched? Our scientists today can take just a few living cells and clone another complete animal from them (albeit, a genetically defective one). Furthermore, even though they don't know how to create life itself yet, they take great pride in the fact that they think they are now on the verge of "creating" life in their laboratories the very near future.

Yet, these same scientists will also religiously tell you that there is no God. They will vehemently argue that randomly, without any designer or purpose, life came into existence and started reproducing all by itself billions of years ago (even though the scientific odds are astronomically high against this ever happening, no matter how much time passes).

Due to advances in medical science, our medical community now knows that (on a limited scale) they can actually breathe life back into a dead person by using mouth to mouth resuscitation, or shock someone back to life using electricity, yet they absolutely refuse to believe that omnipotent God lovingly designed and created the body for the first human being from the dust of the Earth, and then breathed life into that body so that it became a living human being.

We'll talk more about the creation of Adam and his mate Eve in a little bit, but first let's follow along in Genesis to see what God has to say about man's original home and his first vocation.

THE GARDEN OF EDEN- A VERY SPECIAL PLACE

Many people do not realize that the Garden of Eden was a far more extensive and wonderful paradise than even the most magnificent of gardens anywhere in the world today. To begin with, the Bible tells us that the garden was planted by God Himself, and that alone should suggest to us that this was far more glorious than anything man has ever planted since then:

> Then the Lord God planted a garden in Eden in the east, and there he placed the man he had made. The Lord God made all sorts of trees grow up from the ground— trees that were beautiful and that produced delicious fruit. In the middle of the garden he placed the tree of life and the tree of the knowledge of good and evil. Genesis 2: 8-9 NLT

So we see that God placed Adam in the Garden. This was Adam's first home, a garden paradise full of trees of every kind that were beautiful to look at and produced delicious fruit for food. The garden also included two very special trees which we will discuss in a little while. For now, let's continue learning about Eden:

> A river flowed from the land of Eden, watering the garden and then dividing into four branches. The first branch, called the Pishon, flowed around the entire land of Havilah, where gold is found. The gold of that land is exceptionally pure; aromatic resin and onyx stone are also found there. The second branch, called the Gihon, flowed around the entire land of Cush. The third branch, called the Tigris, flowed east of the land of Asshur. The fourth branch is called the Euphrates. Genesis 2:10-14 NLT

Let me once again use some words to paint a mental picture for you in order to describe what our world was like before the destruction in the worldwide flood of Noah's day. The topography of the planet consisted of low mountains and lush valleys interspersed with shallow seas, but there was one spot on Earth which stood out from every other place as being truly magnificent.

The Scriptures suggest that this wonderful paradise was probably the highest point on Earth, a single massive Garden of Eden situated atop a gigantic flat plateau or mesa which certainly covered many acres. It may have even been miles in diameter. We don't know for sure. What the Bible does tell us is that Eden was large enough for a mighty artesian river to flow up through the ground and out from the middle of Eden in four different directions watering the whole Earth before flowing into the seas (another indication that Eden was the highest point on Earth). This is where Adam and Eve lived when they were first created.

GOD'S SECOND STEP IN THE CREATION OF MAN

In the Garden of Eden, man got his first job, caretaking the Garden of God. Yes, God gave man some responsibility. Along with that responsibility, man was free to do whatever he wanted, with only one restriction. God warned man saying "If you eat of the tree of knowledge of good and evil, you will surely die."

Then God gives us another illustrated example of His artistic side. He took some time to demonstrate to Adam and to us that the whole concept of human evolution is nothing more than the product of the foolish and vain imaginations of those who reject the Word of God.

> The Lord God placed the man in the Garden of Eden to tend and watch over it. But the Lord God warned him, "You may freely eat the fruit of every tree in the garden— except the tree of the knowledge of good and evil. If you eat its fruit, you are sure to die." Genesis 2:15-17 NLT
>
> Then the Lord God said, "It is not good for the man to be alone. I will make a helper who is just right for him." So the Lord God formed from the ground all the wild animals and all the birds of the sky. He brought them to the man to see what he would call them, and the man chose a name for each one. He gave names to all the livestock, all the birds of the sky, and all the wild animals. But still there was no helper just right for him. Genesis 2: 18-20 NLT

Here we see God the master artist sitting down to have some fun with Adam. Just like a father amusing their child with play-dough or a master sculptor producing a magnificently beautiful statue, God took lump after lump of earth, forming different birds and animals and giving them life to see what man would give them for a name. Yet, nowhere in the animal kingdom was there a suitable companion and sexual mate for man.

Of course not, because God declares to us that we are a different KIND of being. We are the only life form on Earth created in God's own image and after His likeness. Later on, we'll go into more detail about what God means when He says that we are created in God's own image and likeness. For now, let's take a look at how God solves man's problem of having no mate:

> So the Lord God caused the man to fall into a deep sleep. While the man slept, the Lord God took out one of the man's ribs and closed up the opening. Then the Lord God made a woman from the rib, and he brought her to the man. "At last!" the man exclaimed. "This one is bone from my bone, and flesh from my flesh! She will be called 'woman,' because she was taken from 'man.'" Genesis 2: 21-23 NLT

Let me put this description in scientific terms for those who keep insisting that the Bible is nothing but a bunch of religious superstition. This passage is telling us that God first sedated man so he would not feel any pain. Then God surgically removed one of man's ribs. Then the Lord closed, sealed, and healed the wound. Then God used that rib (bone marrow is excellent for this purpose) and manipulated the chromosomes and other genetics of the living human tissue to clone a biologically female human body from Adam's own DNA.

Eve herself was not a "clone" of Adam. She was a unique human being, a companion created by God, just as Adam was, but her mortal female body was cloned (created) from Adam's biological tissue to be a perfect biological mate for Adam.

Then, when God was finished cloning the biological body for man's mate, He breathed another unique living human soul and spirit into that biological body and brought to man his perfect human mate. Note that

Adam called her "woman" because her body was created from the tissue of his own body.

Eve was never some evolved primate and neither was Adam. They were both complete and perfect human beings, created by God in His own image and likeness and then placed into biological bodies which would enable them to exist and interact with the material world in which they were placed.

One of the goals of Jesus was to teach us that our mortal bodies are not who we are. They are only the biological vessels or "containers" for the beings who live in them. God's Word alludes to our biological bodies as being like houses or temples in which we live. Speaking of His human body and the resurrection of that body, Jesus said "Destroy this temple and in three days, I will raise it up". If you want proof of what I am saying:

> Then answered the Jews and said unto him, What sign shewest thou unto us, seeing that thou doest these things? Jesus answered and said unto them, "Destroy this temple, and in three days I will raise it up." Then said the Jews, Forty and six years was this temple in building, and wilt thou rear it up in three days? But he spake of the temple of his body. John 2:18-21 KJV

Are you following me? Our biological bodies are not human beings. Our bodies only contain and sustain the spiritual beings which God creates and places in the bodies. God created Adam in His own image and likeness and placed him in a biological body that the Lord had created from the Earth itself. God then also created Eve in his own image and likeness and placed her in a biological body that the Lord had created from Adam's own DNA, and all of this is far more "scientific" than any idea that the Evolutionists ever came up with.

GOD'S THIRD STEP IN THE CREATION OF MAN.

It is a serious mistake to suppose that God's participation in the creation of the human race ended with Adam and Eve (the creation of the first man and woman) and from there on the human race has been on our own. The greatest error of all in the philosophies and beliefs of Atheism and secular humanism is in their failure to comprehend that human beings are not independent self-producing biological beings (organisms).

On the contrary, the Bible teaches that God Himself creates every human being. We as human beings are only capable of creating the physical bodies which every new offspring of God will inhabit. In addition, the next Scriptures in Genesis are very important in establishing the truth that God created us to be heterosexual beings.

Farther on in the Scriptures, God explains to us that there is also no validity for racism or national prejudice because the entire human race came from one blood. We all originate from the blood of Adam, the first man.

> "He is the God who made the world and everything in it. Since he is Lord of heaven and earth, he doesn't live in man-made temples, and human hands can't serve his needs—for he has no needs. He himself gives life and breath to everything, and he satisfies every need. From one man he created all the nations throughout the whole earth. He decided beforehand when they should rise and fall, and he determined their boundaries. Acts 17:24-26 NLT

Let us now continue on in the Bible to discover how God further clarifies for us in other places that human beings are a different "kind" of flesh than that of the other animals, who are in turn different in their kinds from each other, again directly refuting the teachings of evolution

> Similarly there are different kinds of flesh—one *kind for humans, another for animals, another for birds, and another for fish.* 1 Corinthians 15:39 NLT

Back in Chapter One of Genesis, we read where God said "Let us make man in our image". Have you ever wondered why God made us? I'll tell you why. It is because God loves company and He loves family. That is why He manifests Himself to us as "Us" (God the Father, God the Son, and God the Holy Spirit).

That is why God created billions and billions of angels, and it is also why God created the human race. That is why God created a "son" whom he named Adam and a "daughter" named Eve. Note that Adam is recorded as God's first human son, his name listed as the first in the record of Jesus Christ's human ancestry in the Book of Luke:

> Which was the son of Enos, which was the son of Seth, which was the son of Adam, which was the son of God. Luke 3:38 KJV

When God uses the word "son" for Adam, it is more than just an endearing term. There is an understanding in Scripture that (from the very beginning) the reason God created man in His own image and called Adam "son" is that God had a desire for family. He wanted to reproduce Himself in perpetuity. God had a desire for His family to continue to exist and increase forever, and that is why God put the Tree of Life in the Garden of Eden.

God's perfect desire was that man would never die, God truly wanted man to live forever. However, God did not create robots with no free will and no capacity to love. God created man with the capacity to love, yet the freedom to reject His Maker and follow someone else's leading, if that is what man desired to do.

It is all the way back in Genesis where Father God begins to clearly lay it out in Scripture for us why it is not in His will for marital relationships to be homosexual (Adam and Steve or Sally and Eve), and it is NOT because God hates homosexuals.

> Therefore a man shall leave his father and mother and be joined to his wife, and they shall become one flesh. Genesis 2: 24 NLT

I often hear preachers talk about this particular Scripture from the perspective of God saying that when a man and a woman come together, it is a matter of two beings joining in marriage to become a single marital unit, the two becoming one "in spirit".

While that is true, there is more to it than this. Just as God took Adam's one flesh and made two people from it, so also does God use the coupling of two people together to produce "one flesh", a human embryo for the next member of God's family. Then God participates in that process of creating a new human being by "breathing" a new spiritual being into that conceived embryo, and about nine months later, another child of God is born into the world.

Yes, listen to me, and think deeply about what the Spirit of God is saying. The third step in the creation of man occurs when every human child is born, because the Scriptures tell us that God directly participates in the birth of every human being. You may not have realized it yet, but the human mother and father only provide the fertilized cell that will become the embryo, the biological body (the temple) for each new human being to inhabit.

The Scriptures tell us that it is God who creates the spiritual being who will inhabit that biological body. By virtue of God's personal participation in the creation of every new human being, we are technically all God's children by virtue of His creation of us, even if most have abandoned our Father in Heaven and are now on the road to following another evil father right into hell.

Once you fully understand and accept this awesome Biblical truth that God is the Father of the whole world, it will help you comprehend why He loves us so much and give you a whole new outlook on the nature and value of all human life from God's perspective, and why God so loved the world that He gave His only begotten Son, so that whosoever believes on Him might be saved.

> "His purpose was for the nations to seek after God and perhaps feel their way toward him and find him— though he is not far from any one of us. For in him we live and move and exist. As some of your own poets have said, 'We are his offspring.' Acts 17: 27-28 NLT

A WORLD WITHOUT EVIL

Let's take a small step back now and have another look at the trees in the Garden of Eden and what they represented. One of the things we learn from the book of Job later on in the Bible is that (even though Satan is a very powerful angelic being) he is incapable of doing anything outside of God's permission. In Job we learn that God does place limitations on the amount of evil Satan can do to humanity, even in our present fallen state.

However, the Bible also tells us that in the beginning when God first created the heavens and the Earth, everything God created on Earth was "very good". As long as Adam and Eve continued to walk in obedience to God, Satan had no permission from God and no power at all to afflict man or man's domain with evil of any kind. The only thing that Satan had the power to do was to talk to Adam and Eve.

As I said before, Adam and Eve were not created as slaves or robots. They were free to believe, trust and obey God and continue to live forever knowing only "very good", or they could choose to believe what Satan told them, disobey God, embrace evil, and freely decide to place themselves under Satan's dominion and rule instead of God's

> ...The tree of life *was also in the midst of the garden, and the tree of the knowledge of good and evil...*The Lord God placed the man in the Garden of Eden to tend and watch over it. But the Lord God warned him, "You may freely eat the fruit of every tree in the garden— except the tree of the knowledge of good and evil. If you eat its fruit, you are sure to die." Genesis 2:9-17 NLT

The Bible does not really tell us exactly how long Adam and Eve were in the Garden of Eden before they disobeyed God and chose to embrace the knowledge of evil. However, there are several indications in the Bible that it may not have been very long at all.

From Genesis 1 we know that before Adam and Eve disobeyed God and ate from the forbidden tree, God had already told Adam and Eve to be fruitful and multiply. Now, most people who are married can remember what it was like when they were newlyweds. Well, there was no evil in the world to hinder Adam and Eve physically coming together as man and wife and nothing to hinder Eve's fertility. Yet Genesis 4 tells us that Eve did not conceive until after they were both sent out from the Garden of Eden. So, this is the first indicator that it was not very long before humanity disobeyed God and ate from the tree of knowledge of good and evil.

Another clue that the time period may have been very short from the time of creation to the time Adam and Eve chose to embrace evil is that (even though they had full access to the tree of life-which was right next to the tree of knowledge of good and evil) they apparently had not eaten from it yet.

We don't know exactly how big the Garden of Eden was, but we do know that the trees of life and the knowledge of evil were close to each other right in the middle of it, and they both stood out as unique from the other trees around them, so they would not have been hard to find. Yet, as soon as Adam and Eve sinned, God evicted them from the Garden of Eden, lest they eat from the tree of life and be condemned to live forever with the knowledge of evil continually corrupting their nature.

> Then the Lord God said, "Look, the human beings have become like us, knowing both good and evil. What if they reach out, take fruit from the tree of life, and eat it? Then they will live forever!" So the Lord God banished them from the Garden of Eden, and he sent Adam out to cultivate the ground from which he had been made. After sending them out, the Lord God stationed mighty cherubim to the east of the Garden of Eden. And he placed a flaming sword that flashed back and forth to guard the way to the tree of life. Genesis 3: 22-24 NLT

So that is the way it went. As soon as Adam and Eve brought evil and sin into mankind's nature, they were banished from Eden and God placed mighty angels at the entrance of Eden. Their flaming swords would prevent anyone from ever entering God's Garden again and eating from the Tree of Life, suggesting that eating from the tree still had the potential to provide eternal life for human beings, even in their sinful state.

Contrary to what many teach, by driving them from the Garden, God was not "punishing" Adam and Eve for their disobedience. God was not angry and condemning them to death by sending them out of the Garden so they couldn't eat from the Tree of Life. God's eviction of Adam and Eve from the Garden of Eden was actually an act of loving mercy.

God created the tree of life to be an eternal blessing for mankind, but when Adam and Eve chose to make evil part of their nature, God's blessing would have become an eternal curse to them. After their rebellion, the Lord did not want His children to eat from the Tree of Life and have evil continually destroying them and consuming all their goodness until they became totally filled with evil for all eternity with no opportunity for redemption just like the fallen angels.

Without death, there would have been no hope for man's salvation. All of humanity would have eventually become just like Satan and his angels, totally evil, with no good left in them. God was not at all willing for that to happen, so Adam and Eve were evicted from the Garden of Eden before they could eat from the Tree of Life.

What happened to The Garden of Eden and the trees in it? Well, Genesis tells us that the flood of Noah's day covered the highest spots on earth to a depth of more than 20 feet. We'll explain how that was possible a little while later, but for now, we'll say that the Garden of Eden and everything in it would have been destroyed in the flood due to the whole world being buried under water for many months and the volcanic upheavals which occurred at the same time.

Let's move on. Let's take a look at this angel Satan, the world's first liar, the same angel whom God identifies as being the one who still deceives the whole world in these end times that we now live in. He is the same angel who will soon be cast out of his present domain of the Second Heaven at the beginning of the Tribulation. Furthermore, when that happens, God's Word tells us that he and his angels will be confined to the First Heaven surrounding Earth and he will come down with great wrath toward God and mankind. He will know that his time of dominion over mankind is almost over, and he will want to steal, destroy and kill, robbing God of as many of His children as possible before Jesus casts Him into the bottomless pit. More to come on that in a few chapters.

CHAPTER 6

Who Was the World's First Liar?

THERE WAS A SPIRIT INSIDE THE SERPENT

To know the answer to this, we need to know our whole Bible, because we do not find out until much later in the Word of God that it was actually Satan who was the invisible angelic being who was concealing his presence within the body of the serpent (or dragon) and speaking through this creature to Eve in an effort to try to convince Adam and Eve to embrace the knowledge of evil.

> The serpent was the shrewdest of all the wild animals the Lord God had made. One day he asked the woman, "Did God really say you must not eat the fruit from any of the trees in the garden?" "Of course we may eat fruit from the trees in the garden," the woman replied. "It's only the fruit from the tree in the middle of the garden that we are not allowed to eat. God said, 'You must not eat it or even touch it; if you do, you will die.'" Genesis 3: 1-3 NLT
> So the great dragon was cast out, that serpent of old, called the Devil and Satan, who deceives the whole world; he was cast to the earth, and his angels were cast out with him. Revelation 12:9 NLT

We already know from the God's Word that (in the beginning) Adam, under God, was the ruler and caretaker of the world and all life on Earth (see Genesis 1:26-28). Furthermore, Satan knew that he was powerless to bring evil into man's domain. He could not do it without man's permission.

Satan did, however, have the freedom and ability to talk to man. Yet, being the coward and deceiver that the Devil is, rather than speak to man directly, Satan chose to disguise his true identity. The Devil convinced the serpent to allow him to enter and speak through the serpent's biological body.

Can Satan and other evil angels co-inhabit and take control of biological beings? Atheists and secular-humanists laugh at the idea, but that is because they have been falsely indoctrinated into the belief that all life forms (including human beings) are strictly biological in nature.

However, the Word of God declares that angels and human beings are actually "spiritual beings" who have an immaterial soul and spirit. Furthermore, God has explained to us in His Word that we only live or "dwell" in these present biological bodies for the first miniscule portion of our eternal existence. Compared to our eternal lives, the Bible tells us that our entire mortal lifespan is less in comparison to a single breath or the blink of an eye.

One of the most important things to understand about spiritual beings is that they don't take up any material space in a biological body. That explains how a single human being can actually house a human spirit and one or many evil spirits at the same time if we are foolish enough to make a habit of deliberately messing with evil things.

There are numerous places throughout the New Testament which tell of Jesus and the disciples casting evil spirits out of many different people, and in at least one instance, Jesus came across a man who had so many demons that they called themselves "Legion". Remember that the New Testament of the Bible was written in Roman times, and at the time of Christ, a "legion" of soldiers could have been anywhere from several hundred to a few thousand.

What we do know is that there were so many demons in this one man that when they left the man and went into a herd of swine, and this is what happened:

For Jesus had already said to the spirit, "Come out of the man, you evil spirit." Then Jesus demanded, "What is your name?" And he replied, "My name is Legion, because there are many of us inside this man." Then the evil spirits begged him again and again not to send them to some distant place. There happened to be a large herd of pigs feeding on the hillside nearby. "Send us into those pigs," the spirits begged. "Let us enter them." So Jesus gave them permission. The evil spirits came out of the man and entered the pigs, and the entire herd of about 2,000 pigs plunged down the steep hillside into the lake and drowned in the water. Mark 5:8-13 NLT

Therefore, the Word of God is very clear that it is possible for more than one spiritual being to inhabit a single biological body at the same time, and this goes for both animal and human bodies.

On the positive side of this disturbing reality, Jesus promised His disciples that once He was resurrected and had ascended to Father God, He would send the Holy Spirit down to Earth to make His home with anyone who loved God and wanted to be filled with the Holy Spirit of God.

The good news is that if we are filled with the Holy Spirit, no devil or demon can get in as long as we do not turn away from the Spirit of God and open the door for it to happen. So, if we welcome the Holy Spirit into our being and live for God, we never need to fear being "possessed" by any evil spirit. They certainly have the ability to externally torment and tempt or try to influence Christians for a time, as they did Jesus, but they cannot take control of us if we are filled with, and walking in obedience to the Spirit of God.

So let's leave you with the promise of God that if we are filled with the Holy Spirit and living for God, we never need to fear being taken over and possessed by any demon. They might attack us from the outside, but they cannot inhabit those in whom God fully resides. Through Christ, you are more than conquerors of Satan, and he no longer has any right or power to enter your body.

Now, let's learn a little more about this angelic being called Lucifer, who became Satan. We just read in Revelation that Satan is metaphorically called both a dragon and a serpent. From the description given in Genesis regarding God's sentence upon the serpent for allowing Satan to use him in this way (e.g. from that time on, serpents would crawl on their bellies in the dust) it seems that when serpents were originally created, they had limbs as other creatures did.

Then succeeding generations of serpents genetically lost those limbs as a consequence of what the original serpent allowed Satan to do. Perhaps this is where the legends of dragons originated. As mentioned before, the Book of Job may actually be the oldest book in the Bible, and in the book of Job, God speaks of just such a limbed serpentine creature.

> "I want to emphasize Leviathan's limbs and its enormous strength and graceful form. Who can strip off its hide, and who can penetrate its double layer of armor? Who could pry open its jaws? For its teeth are terrible! The scales on its back are like rows of shields tightly sealed together. They are so close together that no air can get between them. Each scale sticks tight to the next. They interlock and cannot be penetrated. "When it sneezes, it flashes light! Its eyes are like the red of dawn. Lightning leaps from its mouth; flames of fire flash out. Smoke streams from its nostrils like steam from a pot heated over burning rushes. Its breath would kindle coals, for flames shoot from its mouth. Job 41:12-21 NLT

Wow! Let me tell you here and now that you might as well ignore the footnotes and modern translations of unlearned men who suggest that this creature was a crocodile. It is not like any crocodile we know. If you read the whole chapter, God even goes into a lot more detail regarding this amazing dragon beast that breathed fire. What a magnificent dragon creature Leviathan must have been! Yet they are now extinct, and the Word of God tells us why.

> So the Lord God said to the serpent: "Because you have done this, you *are* cursed more than all cattle, and more than every beast of the field. On your belly you shall

go, and you shall eat dust all the days of your life. Genesis
3:14 NLT

So, the serpent or dragon eventually lost his limbs for his part in co-
operating with Satan and his evil plot against humanity, and the creature
itself became extinct at some point after the flood, just as behemoth did.
Let's go back now to Adam and Eve's encounter with Satan in the Garden
of Eden and listen as he speaks to them through the mouth of the serpent
dragon.

THE FATHER OF ALL LIES AND LIARS

God certainly hit the nail on the head when he renamed Lucifer,
calling him "Satan" (meaning false accuser). The first thing that comes
out of Satan's mouth when he encounters Eve in the Garden of Eden is
an accusatory question, suggesting God was forbidding them to eat from
any of the trees in the Garden. Concealing himself within the Serpent's
body, the Devil used this lying tactic as a gauge to determine how well
Eve knew God's Word. Satan was looking for a weakness, and it was not
long before he found one.

> The serpent was the shrewdest of all the wild animals
> the Lord God had made. One day he asked the woman,
> "Did God really say you must not eat the fruit from any
> of the trees in the garden?" "Of course we may eat fruit
> from the trees in the garden," the woman replied. "It's only
> the fruit from the tree in the middle of the garden that we
> are not allowed to eat. God said, 'You must not eat it or
> even touch it; if you do, you will die.'" Genesis 3:1-3 NLT

So, first we have the accusation in the form of a question. "Is God
forbidding you to eat from all of the trees in the Garden?" Then we have
Eve's correct answer. "We can eat from all of the trees except one". Next
(however innocently) Eve ADDS TO the Word of God by stating that God
had said that if they even TOUCHED it, they would die.

As soon as Eve made that statement, Satan knew that he had a window of opportunity which he could exploit to possibly turn mankind against God. You see, Eve had not yet been created when God gave instructions to Adam regarding the tree of knowledge of good and evil, but Satan was around, and he knew exactly what God had said. Satan knew that God had not said anything at all about people dying from merely touching the tree or its fruit:

> But the Lord God warned him, "You may freely eat the fruit of every tree in the garden— except the tree of the knowledge of good and evil. If you eat its fruit, you are sure to die." Genesis 2: 16-17 NLT

It doesn't really matter where Eve came up with the false idea, the belief that she would die from touching the tree or its fruit. Maybe it was her own idea, or maybe Adam loved her so much that he warned her not to even touch the tree in case she died. What does matter is that Eve had developed a mistaken belief. God did not say that touching the tree would result in death, and Satan was crafty and deceitful enough to take advantage of Eve's false belief.

Satan was sly enough to realize that if he lied to Eve and created a great enough desire in her where she would be tempted to actually touch the tree, handle the fruit and pick the fruit, NOTHING WOULD HAPPEN. Why? Well, nothing would happen because God had not said that they would die just from touching the fruit.

Yet, Satan knew that Eve had somehow developed the BELIEF that God had said they would die from touching the fruit. Therefore, if she picked the fruit and nothing happened, Eve would be tempted to doubt God's truthfulness. Then she might possibly go to the next step of disobeying God and actually eating the fruit (which God had said surely WOULD bring about her death). Of course, God's Word reveals that Satan's devious plan was successful, and with his deception, Satan managed to convince Eve to disobey God and eat the fruit.

> "You won't die!" the serpent replied to the woman.
> "God knows that your eyes will be opened as soon as you

eat it, and you will be like God, knowing both good and evil." The woman was convinced. She saw that the tree was beautiful and its fruit looked delicious, and she wanted the wisdom it would give her. So she took some of the fruit and ate it. Then she gave some to her husband, who was with her, and he ate it, too. Genesis 3: 4-6 NLT

Once again, we have a small passage of Scripture containing some very important details if you want to understand how Satan works in human society. We already took a look at Satan's oldest lie in the world, which is essentially "God is keeping something good from you. He does not want you to enjoy life."

Now Satan adds two more lies to his deception. The second lie is that man would not die from eating from the tree of knowledge of good and evil. The third lie is that embracing the knowledge of evil would make man like God. In the KJV, it says "your eyes shall be opened and ye shall be as gods". In other words, Satan was telling Adam and Eve that embracing the knowledge of evil would enable them to "evolve into gods".

I don't care what anyone else says. I am telling you the truth when I say to you that there are no other gods in outer space. There are no advanced alien civilizations who have "evolved" independently of God somewhere else in the universe. They are all the inventions of devils and demons who want the foolish of humanity to accept and welcome devils when they manifest themselves in physical form.

Don't think that this is not going to happen after the bride of Christ is gone. The Bible has plenty of examples of "good" angels (such as Gabriel) appearing in visible form to encourage people toward God, and the only thing that is hindering evil angels from doing the same thing to draw people to Satan is that the Holy Spirit is presently hindering it from happening.

God tells us in the book of Genesis that one of the great evils before and after the flood of Noah was that evil angels were manifesting their presence in the world and taking possession of people for violent and sexual purposes, and once the Bride of Christ and the Holy Spirit are taken out of the way, the same thing will once again be happening again on a pandemic level worldwide during the seven year Tribulation.

Just preceding the coming Tribulation when the Bride of Christ and the Holy Spirit are caught up, the Bible tells us that Satan and his evil followers will once again go to war with God and his angels (perhaps in an attempt to prevent Christ from coming for His Bride) and this time, when Satan and his followers are defeated, they will be cast out of their present realm in outer space (the Second Heaven), and for the last seven years of the Devil's rule on Earth, they will all be further confined to dwell in the area immediately around Earth's atmospheric heaven, the First Heaven.

Satan and the angels who follow him are going to be furious when they lose again against God and they will take it out on mankind with a vengeance because they all know this will signal that their time ruling Earth will shortly be coming to an end.

As far as mankind goes, for those who remain on Earth, this period of human history will be even worse than it was in the time of the flood. Demon possession is going to be rampant throughout the human race. Even though there will be no worldwide flood, the spread of evil will become so bad globally that the Bible declares to us:

> For there will be greater anguish than at any time
> since the world began. And it will never be so great again.
> In fact, unless that time of calamity is shortened, not a
> single person will survive. But it will be shortened for the
> sake of God's chosen ones. Matthew 24:21-22 NLT

God is not telling us this so that we live in terror of what is coming. Rather God is calling us to come to Him. God loves us and he is warning us that it will be Satan who is bringing all this evil and suffering upon the human race. The truth is that God wants us to be with Him in Heaven during this time, and He clearly shows us how to be saved from all of this coming death and destruction:

> Peter replied, "Each of you must repent of your sins
> and turn to God, and be baptized in the name of Jesus
> Christ for the forgiveness of your sins. Then you will
> receive the gift of the Holy Spirit. This promise is to you,
> to your children, and to those far away—all who have

been called by the Lord our God." Then Peter continued preaching for a long time, strongly urging all his listeners, "Save yourselves from this crooked generation!" Those who believed what Peter said were baptized and added to the church that day—about 3,000 in all. Acts 2:38-41 NLT

Dear readers, beloved of God, who are you going to believe, our Father in Heaven or the father of all lies and liars? I hope and pray that every person reading this book who is not already a believer will come to a saving knowledge of Jesus Christ as our Lord and Redeemer during or after reading this book.

Contrary to what some teach, God wants us ALL in Heaven as the Bride of Christ during the seven year Tribulation of pouring out of wrath on the rebellious and wicked remnant of mankind. What kind of loving Father or loving Bridegroom would want their beloved suffering through the last seven years of Satan's reign while the Devil creates hell on Earth for a wicked and rebellious generation ruled by the Antichrist and the False Prophet?

Yes, I know there are some who dispute a pre-tribulation resurrection, claiming with false humility that it is vain to think that we deserve to be spared suffering for Christ when many have been suffering for Jesus all around the world ever since Christianity began. What foolish talk! What you are saying is that God wants every Christian in the world to be persecuted, tortured and killed during the last seven years, and out of the goodness of His heart, God will spare a few of us. God certainly does not want that.

The resurrection will not occur because we as Christians in the free world are any more deserving of being spared persecution and suffering than those who are now already being attacked worldwide. It will occur because God has a time and place for everything, and it is Father God (not Christians) who will decide when Christ will come.

Mankind is already killing millions of God's children every year through abortion, terrorism and genocide. We are already living in the shadow of the seven year tribulation, yet not every Christian in historical existence has had to suffer and die for Jesus, and we should be grateful that we are now enjoying God's blessings because of the faithfulness of previous generations of men and women of God in our nations.

However, the whole world today is increasingly being caught up in spiritual and biological whoredom. Evil worldwide is rapidly reaching the disgusting level where God is about to declare that "IT IS ENOUGH", the cup of evil is full. His angels are about to sound a trumpet calling on the body of Christ to come up to heaven so that this world can be given over to Satan for his last seven years, and those seven years are going to be hell on Earth, getting progressively worse with each passing year.

God does not want us here during that. That is why His Holy Spirit (speaking through those who love God) continues to call mankind to repentance and faith in Jesus Christ. God wants us to be part of the wedding party of Jesus, not part of Satan's insane seven year attempt to eradicate and enslave all of mankind before he is removed from the scene and imprisoned for the first thousand years of Christ's kingdom rule on Earth.

You see, the flood of Noah's day was not for the righteous. It was immediate judgement upon the wicked with virtually no opportunity for repentance and salvation. Likewise, the 7 year tribulation not a "test" for the righteous. It too is a judgement upon the wicked, but unlike the flood, God will give humanity seven final years of unrestrained wrathful rulership under Satan with the desire that, once humanity has tasted evil of this magnitude, at least some will turn back to God and be saved, if not in life, then in death.

God even tells us why the Tribulation will continue to worsen during the second half of the tribulation, even after billions have already died during the first half. It is not because the faith of today's Christians will need to be "tested" to the death. God tells us that the Tribulation will continue because:

> the rest of the men which were not killed by these plagues yet repented not of the works of their hands, that they should not worship devils, and idols of gold, and silver, and brass, and stone, and of wood: which neither can see, nor hear, nor walk: Neither repented they of their

murders, nor of their sorceries, nor of their fornication, nor of their thefts. Revelation 9: 20-21 KJV

Dear friends, Satan wants to destroy every one of us, but God's will for us is to repent and go with Christ when He comes for those who love Him. Then God says that we will return with Jesus when he comes back to Earth to put a stop to the insanity.

What shall we do, then? Should we follow Christ into Heaven or follow Satan into the Tribulation and Lake of Fire? The smart choice is a no-brainer. Let us together do the wise thing and repent now, believe on Jesus Christ now, follow and obey Him now, and we shall not be ashamed at His coming.

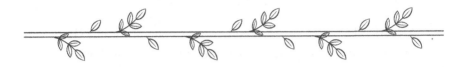

CHAPTER 7

There Are 3 Basic Types of Sin

THE THREE TEMPTATIONS OF LIFE

Evil is not really all that complicated when you look at it in its three basic forms. In the New Testament, the Apostle John talks about three basic temptations that are common to all of us:

> For the world offers only a craving for physical pleasure, a craving for everything we see, and pride in our achievements and possessions. These are not from the Father, but are from this world. 1 John 2: 16 NLT

In the KJV, the Bible describes these three basic temptations as the **lust of the eyes, the lust of the flesh, and pride,** and we see that all three temptations were present in the Garden of Eden.

1. First Eve focuses the tree's beauty with her eyes (lust, desire)
2. Then Eve wants it for food, even though she has a huge variety of food and no need for this fruit (flesh, greed)
3. Last of all, she thinks it will make her wise, help her evolve into a god. (pride, vanity)

Many people do not realize that, even though the circumstances were much different, Satan used these very same basic temptations to try to trick Jesus Christ into sinning when the Devil tempted Christ in the wilderness:

1. The lust of the flesh

   And when the tempter came to him, he said: If thou be the Son of God, command that these stones be made bread. Matthew 4:3 KJV

2. The lust of the eyes

   Again, the devil taketh him up into an exceeding high mountain, and showed him all the kingdoms of the world, and the glory of them; And said unto him, All these things will I give thee, if thou wilt fall down and worship me. Matthew 4: 8-9 KJV

3. The pride of life

   Then the devil taketh him up into the holy city, and setteth him on a pinnacle of the temple, And saith unto him, If thou be the Son of God, cast thyself down: for it is written, He shall give his angels charge concerning thee: and in their hands they shall bear thee up, lest at any time thou dash thy foot against a stone. Matthew 4: 5-6 KJV

In addition, the Scriptures tell us that none of us suffers temptations that are not common to all other people, and if you really think about it, even though the circumstances may vary greatly, every sin in existence falls within one of these three basic categories. In each of them, we have all failed God at one time or another. Therefore, I thank God today that where Adam and Eve failed and where we too sometimes fail and succumb to temptation, Jesus Christ remained loving, faithful and true to Father God, remembering that the Father sent Him to Earth to remain sinless for the sake of mankind's redemption, and an important detail to remember is that Jesus defeated Satan's twisting of the Word of God by quoting and obeying the true Word of God.

DON'T BLAME EVE FOR THE FALL OF HUMANITY

I sometimes come across men in particular who try to support their false opinion of women as being inferior to men, or justify their poor treatment of women by "passing the buck" and saying that the human race would not be in the trouble we are in now if Eve had not eaten from the forbidden tree. "It's all her fault", they say.

What an evil thing to think and say. We can never justify our own wickedness by blaming it on someone else. It only proves that we are evil when we try to do this. In the Garden of Eden, Eve tried to blame the serpent, Adam tried to blame both Eve and God, and many people still do exactly the same thing today. We tend to blame everyone but ourselves for our sin.

> The man replied, "It was the woman you gave me who gave me the fruit, and I ate it." Then the Lord God asked the woman, "What have you done?" The serpent deceived me," she replied. "That's why I ate it." Genesis 3: 12-13 NLT

Yes, even though Eve was the first to believe the lie, disobey God and embrace evil, the Bible tells us that God did NOT hold Eve responsible for the fall of humanity because she had INDEED been deceived, so if the Lord Himself does not blame women for the fall of man, isn't it foolish and evil for us to do so?

Now, listen my dear male friends. It is time to address the elephant in the room. I am referring to the fact that God had spoken DIRECTLY to Adam before Eve was created, warning him not to eat from the fruit of the forbidden tree. God held Adam responsible for his own welfare, and for that of his wife, and the important factor in the responsibility equation is this. As we just finished reading a short time ago, when Eve picked the fruit and ate it, ADAM WAS RIGHT THERE WITH HER listening to everything the Serpent said.

> ...Then she gave some to her husband, who was with her, and he ate it, too. Genesis 3: 6 NLT

You see, Adam was not deceived. He knew exactly what God had said. Yet, when Eve took of the fruit and ate it, he did not try to warn or stop her. Then, when she did eat from the tree without any immediate visible consequences, Adam could still have refused to eat the fruit himself. Adam was still guiltless at that point, until he chose to doubt God, believe the Devil, and disobey God by yielding to his wife's temptation that he should also embrace the knowledge of evil.

Then, from that moment on, everything changed in Adam and Eve's world. They had both voluntarily removed themselves from God's protection and willingly subjugated themselves to Satan (the one whom they had chosen to obey) without realizing that Satan's ultimate plan was to corrupt them and destroy their mortal bodies. Satan wanted to kill them and then continue to dominate their souls and spirits forever, subjecting them to an eternity of torment in hell.

For those who think that it will be God and His angels (and not Satan and his angels) who will be the cause of torment in hell and the Lake of fire, I must say that you have a wrong concept of God, and we will talk about that later. Right now let's leave that alone and take a look at how the Scriptures reveal that Adam and Eve immediately lost something very precious when they disobeyed God, and how Satan used that loss to bring fear and shame into their lives.

> And the eyes of them both were opened, and they
> knew that they were naked; and they sewed fig leaves
> together, and made themselves aprons. Genesis 3:7 KJV

Some people will suggest that up to this point Adam and Eve were ignorant of their nudity, and when they embraced evil, all of a sudden they became ashamed of their nudity and that's why they made aprons of leaves. No! No! No! There is much more going on here than just Adam and Eve starting out physically naked and then covering up with leaves because they suddenly realized that they were naked. God created them innocent, not stupid.

In order to understand the full dynamic of what occurred at the moment of Adam and Eve's rebellion against God, it is important for us to understand that in Adam and Eve's original created nature, there was

NO SIN. There was no darkness. There was NO EVIL at all. Everything about them was "very good".

This is a very significant detail because we see an important difference between God's original interaction with Adam and Eve before sin entered their being, and God's interaction with Adam and Eve and all of their descendants until now after evil became part of human nature, and it directly involves the evil that has become a part of human nature ever since Adam made it so. When Adam and Eve chose to embrace evil, there was something extremely important in their being that had to "leave" in order for the evil to come in and become part of their nature.

SIN CANNOT SURVIVE GOD'S GLORY

One of the valuable truths which we can learn from the encounter between God and Moses on Mount Sinai is that when Moses expressed a desire to see God in all His glory, God explained to Moses that mankind's biological bodies in our present corrupted state cannot endure or survive God's fully glorified presence:

> The Lord replied to Moses, "I will indeed do what you have asked, for I look favorably on you, and I know you by name." Moses responded, "Then show me your glorious presence." The Lord replied, "I will make all my goodness pass before you, and I will call out my name, Yahweh, before you. For I will show mercy to anyone I choose, and I will show compassion to anyone I choose. But you may not look directly at my face, for no one may see me and live." The Lord continued, "Look, stand near me on this rock. As my glorious presence passes by, I will hide you in the crevice of the rock and cover you with my hand until I have passed by. Then I will remove my hand and let you see me from behind. But my face will not be seen." Exodus 33: 17-23 NLT

Yet, we see here that God did consent to give Moses a small taste of how wonderful it will be in the New Heaven and Earth when evil is totally eradicated from the Kingdom of God and the Glory of God fills His entire Kingdom to the point where there is no longer any need of the sun during the day nor the moon and stars at night. In the new Heavens and Earth there will be no more night and no more darkness anywhere in the kingdom of God because God's glory will actually shine forth from the beings of every resident of the new heavens and the new Earth.

> And the city has no need of sun or moon, for the glory of God illuminates the city, and the Lamb is its light. The nations will walk in its light, and the kings of the world will enter the city in all their glory. Its gates will never be closed at the end of day because there is no night there. And all the nations will bring their glory and honor into the city. Revelation 21:23-26 NLT

God also gives us a little taste of what our appearance is going to be like in the future by the Bible's description of the change in the appearance of Moses after experiencing just a little bit of God's glory when God passed by, and Moses got to see God's back portion.

> When Moses came down Mount Sinai carrying the two stone tablets inscribed with the terms of the covenant, he wasn't aware that his face had become radiant because he had spoken to the Lord. So when Aaron and the people of Israel saw the radiance of Moses' face, they were afraid to come near him. Exodus 34: 29-30 NLT

What we are seeing here is that when Moses was exposed directly to only a small portion of God's glorified presence, God's Glory was actually absorbed into Moses' being and was then reflected out again. The absorbed glory of God radiated out from Moses so greatly that when he came down from the mountain, Israel was afraid to look directly at Moses, and he had to cover his face with a veil until the Glory of God faded after a while.

We have an even more spectacular example of how much of God's Glory that a SINLESS human body is capable of enduring and radiating in Matthew 17, where Jesus takes His three closest disciples with Him up a high mountain away from other people, and there Jesus allows God's glory to shine out from His human body:

> Six days later Jesus took Peter and the two brothers, James and John, and led them up a high mountain to be alone. As the men watched, Jesus' appearance was transformed so that his face shone like the sun, and his clothes became as white as light. Matthew 17: 1-2 NLT

Many teach that this was an example of Jesus revealing His Deity, but that is not really an accurate description of what happened on that day. This was a revelation by Jesus to His disciples, (and to all of us) of what a SINLESS human being really looks like with God's Glory radiating out from their mortal body. None of the common artist's conceptions of Adam, Eve and God in the Garden of Eden are really accurate (including the cover of this book).

What Peter, James and John saw on the Mount of Transfiguration is not only what "The Word" would have looked like in the Garden of Eden. It is what Adam and Eve looked like when they were originally created by God in the Garden of Eden. As they were sinless at the time and dwelling directly in the presence of God, they would have been "clothed" with the same kind of GLORY that exuded from Jesus when he temporarily allowed it to shine forth from His being.

ADAM AND EVE WERE NOT UNCOVERED

What I am telling you is that Christ's transfiguration is a glimpse of what we will look like in the future after the resurrection and it is what Adam and Eve originally looked like. The reason that the Heavenly Jerusalem will no longer need the sun, moon and stars is because the glorious light emanating from our resurrected human bodies will be the light of it. Through these Scriptures, we can understand that, even though Adam and Eve were physically naked when they were created in the beginning, they were most certainly not uncovered in their sinless state, for God's glory was their covering.

In the beginning, Adam and Eve had no material clothing, but they were created in the direct presence of God and walked and talked with God while they were sinless. Consequently, when Adam and Eve were first created, they were "infused" and "clothed" with an even greater absorbed Glory than Moses manifested when he came down from talking with God, for we must remember that even Moses was not without sin.

God warned Moses that he would not survive God's full presence, but Adam and Eve were SINLESS in the beginning, and God walked and talked with them. The Glory of Adam and Eve in their original state was the same type of Glory that Jesus manifested when He was transfigured on the mountain.

Listen to me, dear readers. In the beginning, there was no evil in the nature of Adam and Eve and no sin in their lives. When Adam and Eve walked and talked in the Garden with God the Word, there was no doubt in the mind of any creature in Heaven or Earth that this was the son and daughter of God.

Everywhere they went, they were "clothed" with the Glory of God radiating forth from their entire being, shining like the sun so brightly that it could be seen from afar. Every creature understood that these were God's offspring, His children, created in the very image and likeness of God, the rulers of the entire Earth, more glorious in their appearance even than the angels.

Some have suggested that Adam and Eve were originally naked and unashamed because they were ignorant of what nakedness was, and then once evil entered their thinking, they started to think of nakedness as being evil, so they became ashamed of their nakedness and tried to cover their nakedness with clothing made from leaves. No, dear friends. That is not what happened.

In the beginning, Adam and Eve were so filled with the Glory of God from being in His presence that their bodies brilliantly radiated God's Glory, and the Glory of God was their covering. God's Glory was their clothing. But when Adam and Eve chose to embrace the knowledge of evil and make evil part of their being, God's infilling Glory had to leave in order to make room for the darkness of evil to come in.

> For You *are* not a God who takes pleasure in wickedness, Nor shall evil dwell with You. Psalm 5:4 NKJV

> At that moment their eyes were opened, and they suddenly felt shame at their nakedness. So they sewed fig leaves together to cover themselves. Genesis 3: 7 NLT

Oh what a tragedy! Oh what agonizing sorrow and shame they must have felt! They had chosen to reject God and embrace evil, and now their covering, the Glory of God was gone, and there would be no hiding what they had done.

Adam and Eve were now ashamed of their nakedness. In the world's first example of "false religion", they tried to cover themselves with leaves, and for the first time in their lives, they were afraid of God. Why? Because "fear" and "shame" and "condemnation" are weapons that Satan uses to manipulate his subjects in his dominion of evil. He wants man to fear God and believe that God is angry and tyrannical, always ready to punish, even condemn and kill mankind for our disobedience. But that is not the God I know. That is not the real God. That is not the God who so loved the world that He sent His Son to die for us.

> When the cool evening breezes were blowing, the man and his wife heard the Lord God walking about in the garden. So they hid from the Lord God among the trees. Then the Lord God called to the man, "Where are you?" He replied, "I heard you walking in the garden, so I hid. I was afraid because I was naked." Genesis 3:8-10 NLT

ADAM AND EVE PLAY THE BLAME GAME

Whenever humans are caught sinning, one of the most common excuses mankind uses is to try to shift the blame for our sin away from ourselves and on to another person or thing. "I stole, or was violent because

I was drunk or stoned". "Somebody else made me do it." "I was unfaithful, but it was because someone else tempted me."

> "Who told you that you were naked?" the Lord God asked. "Have you eaten from the tree whose fruit I commanded you not to eat?" The man replied, "It was the woman you gave me who gave me the fruit, and I ate it." Then the Lord God asked the woman, "What have you done?" "The serpent deceived me," she replied. "That's why I ate it." Genesis 3: 11-13 NLT

Every one of us has all kinds of lame excuses for our sin, and so did Adam and Eve. Adam blamed God and Eve. Then Eve blamed the serpent, yet deep down we know that they are all lies. The truth is that we are ALL responsible for our own behavior.

Yet God was merciful to Eve because her knowledge of what God had said was second-hand (from Adam), and the serpent had also lied, and contradicted what Adam had told her. Therefore, the responsibility for the fall of humanity would rest on Adam's shoulders, not Eve's. Adam was not deceived. He was unbelieving. He rejected God's Word, turned His back on God, and chose to believe Satan instead.

We already discussed the fact that God was also not pleased with the serpent allowing Satan to conceal himself within the serpent's body in order to perform his deception. God decreed that the serpent would lose the use of his limbs for this infraction. Yet apparently, even the serpent will receive mercy in the end, as the Scriptures talk about children playing in the serpent's den in Christ's millennial kingdom and beyond without ever coming to harm.

However, included in God's judgement of the serpent, the Lord also pronounced a prophecy about what was going to happen in the future regarding the struggle between man and Satan (the angelic being who was concealing his presence within the serpent's body and was ultimately the one responsible for all of this):

> And I will cause hostility between you and the woman, and between your offspring and her offspring.

He will strike your head, and you will strike his heel."
Genesis 3:15 NLT

The gist of what God is saying here is that there would be an ongoing conflict between Satan and mankind that would continue throughout all of Eve's offspring and continue to cause mankind harm. Yet, God gave Adam and Eve a promise of hope. Even though Satan will be able to hurt her offspring, speaking of all humanity (but particularly of Jesus Christ), in the end, her descendant (Jesus) will crush the serpent's (Satan's) head.

Now in the next chapter, we come to the biggest question of this book. Who Really Killed Adam and Eve?

CHAPTER 8

Did God Kill Adam and Eve?

WHO REALLY KILLED ADAM AND EVE?

Now we come to the main theme of this book and my responsibility to give a sound Biblical explanation as to how God is a God of light, love and life, and not a god of darkness, destruction and death. The answer to the question of who killed Adam and Eve is really very easy to find in the Bible if you know where to look, and yet many people will give the wrong answer to the question because they don't really know their Bible and even though they know a little about God, they do not really know His Spirit or feel the heart of God.

On top of that, Satan has plenty of people around who are willing to blame God for every evil calamity in the world including sickness and death, just the way Adam tried to blame God for his sin in the Garden of Eden. The Devil desperately wants all mankind to continue to be deceived into thinking and believing that it was "God" who punished and killed Adam and Eve. The truth is that mankind is much easier for Satan to further deceive if we are already believing a lie.

This is the place in the book where all those who want you to believe that God is a God of rage and violence and that the Bible is a book of contradiction and condemnation will bang their fist on the table and point to the Scriptures which declare that God creates evil and God destroyed all mankind in the flood (women and children included) and ordered Israel to slaughter all of their enemies, including the innocent women and children.

They'll argue about how all religions (including Christianity) are at the root of many wars and a multitude of other evils. They'll expose past atrocities where professing Christians did this evil and did that evil, and they'll point out in the Bible where God says:

> I form the light, and create darkness: I make peace, and create evil: I the Lord do all these things. Isaiah 45:7 KJV

So, how do we reconcile Scriptures like this (along with the historical record of the Bible and human society) with the promise in the Bible that God is our kind and merciful and forgiving and longsuffering Father in Heaven who dearly loves every one of us without measure?

The key to understanding the relationship between good and evil and the dynamics between God and Satan is once again all carefully laid out for us in the Bible. More specifically, it is clearly outlined in the Book of Job, one of the oldest books of the Bible. Yet, most people only know enough about Job to be able to suggest that the book is God's example to us that we should be faithful to God even though He wants us suffer for our own good and permits a lot of evil to happen to us.

Not only is this a warped perspective on what happened to Job, it also totally misses the primary purpose for the book of Job being written in the first place by portraying God as the culprit in mankind's sufferings. This is exactly what Satan wants us to believe. This allows Satan to remain invisibly working in the background to steal, destroy and kill amidst the human race while God gets the blame for everything Satan does.

GOD IS MAN'S BENEFACTOR AND PROTECTOR

The book of Job begins by telling us that there once was a God-fearing man named Job who loved God, avoided evil and was in the habit of regularly praying to God for his family of ten children (Job 1:1-5). Right after this, we see a very interesting Scripture:

> Now there was a day when the sons of God came to
> present themselves before the Lord, and Satan came also
> among them. Job 1: 6 KJV

Among professing Christians, there are a few differing opinions regarding what this Scripture actually means. Some think it is referring to the spirits of deceased believers such as Abraham coming before God.

I do not think that this is correct, because there are many other Scriptures in the Bible which indicate that, until Jesus Christ was resurrected, all the spirits of deceased believers were confined to the "Paradise" compartment of Hades (the place of the dead) where they were comforted and protected by God, but they were unable to leave.

They were not in heaven yet and could not go there until Christ's death. Before Christ's resurrection, all of the dead were protected, but still within the dominion of Satan. They could not leave because Jesus Christ had not yet paid the price for man's redemption and release from Satan's ruling power.

I believe that what the Word of God is telling us here is that, even though angels were not created in the image and likeness of God in the same relationship that we have with God, the Lord still regards the angels as His "sons" in the sense that God "created" all of them.

Here in Job is where God reveals to us that all angels, good and evil are required to report their activity to God on a regular basis, and on this particular day, Satan was present, along with the angelic sons of God who were reporting their activities to the Lord:

> Now there was a day when the sons of God came to
> present themselves before the Lord, and Satan also came
> among them. And the Lord said to Satan, "From where do
> you come?" So Satan answered the Lord and said, "From
> going to and fro on the earth, and from walking back and
> forth on it." Job 1: 6-7 NKJV

Next we see that Job was a man who pleased God. God loved Job, and had blessed and protected him and his family from Satan for his whole life. You see, God is not our punisher and killer. He is our Savior and protector.

> Then the Lord asked Satan, "Have you noticed my servant Job? He is the finest man in all the earth. He is blameless—a man of complete integrity. He fears God and stays away from evil." Satan replied to the Lord, "Yes, but Job has good reason to fear God. You have always put a wall of protection around him and his home and his property. You have made him prosper in everything he does. Look how rich he is! But reach out and take away everything he has, and he will surely curse you to your face!" Job 1: 8-11 NLT

Notice here that Satan challenges God to take away everything from Job. Satan wanted to hurt God and he wanted to hurt Job. Satan knew that hurting Job would bring God great sorrow, and to compound his evil act, Satan also wanted God to get the blame for it all.

Nevertheless, to prove to Satan that Job was indeed a godly man and a true son of God (a shadow of Jesus Christ), Father God agrees to remove His protection from Job for a time. Yet, God Himself <u>does not do anything at all to Job</u>. Satan is the one who would be bringing all of the evil into Job's life, and furthermore, God still places a limit on the evil that Satan do:

> And the Lord said to Satan, "Behold, all that he has *is* in your power; only do not lay a hand on his *person*."
> Job 1:12 NKJV

It is important to understand here that God lays the blame for what happens next squarely in Satan's lap (where it belongs) and God still sets boundaries for Satan that the Devil has no authority or power to pass over. "I am giving you the responsibility for Job's welfare, but you are not permitted to harm him personally."

JOB LOSES HIS WEALTH AND HIS CHILDREN

Now, we've all had bad days, but not many people in the free world have ever had to endure a day like this one. In a single day, Job gets news that most of His wealth has been wiped out and his workers (many who would have also been his friends) were all dead:

> One day when Job's sons and daughters were feasting at the oldest brother's house, a messenger arrived at Job's home with this news: "Your oxen were plowing, with the donkeys feeding beside them, when the Sabeans raided us. They stole all the animals and killed all the farmhands. I am the only one who escaped to tell you." While he was still speaking, another messenger arrived with this news: "The fire of God has fallen from heaven and burned up your sheep and all the shepherds. I am the only one who escaped to tell you." While he was still speaking, a third messenger arrived with this news: "Three bands of Chaldean raiders have stolen your camels and killed your servants. I am the only one who escaped to tell you." Job 1: 13-17 NLT

Take note that in each case, Satan leaves one person alive so that there is someone who will come back to Job and bring him all of the bad news. Also note that even though Satan has done all of this and God has done nothing, one of the surviving servants makes a specific point of blaming God for what happened. Then, as if this tragedy wasn't hurtful enough, on the same day, someone else comes running in with even worse bad news:

> While he was still speaking, another messenger arrived with this news: "Your sons and daughters were feasting in their oldest brother's home. Suddenly, a powerful wind swept in from the wilderness and hit the house on all sides. The house collapsed, and all your children are dead. I am the only one who escaped to tell you." Job 1: 18-19 NLT

Here again we have Satan sparing one lone person to return right away to Job and heap more sorrow on his heart by telling him of all this. Imagine what it would be like to lose all of your wealth and livelihood, have many of your friends murdered, and suffer the loss of all of your children on a single day. There are many people today who would blame God and turn away from God for much less than this, and yet Job still would not sin, deny God, or accuse God of wrongdoing when tempted to do so, not even when his own wife tries to convince him to "curse God and die." (Job 2:9)

> Job stood up and tore his robe in grief. Then he shaved his head and fell to the ground to worship. He said, "I came naked from my mother's womb, and I will be naked when I leave. The Lord gave me what I had, and the Lord has taken it away. Praise the name of the Lord!" In all of this, Job did not sin by blaming God. Job 1: 20-22 NLT

Job is the picture of true spiritual maturity in a believer. So many people today are quick to blame and accuse God for everything that happens on Earth and in their own lives without really understanding the dynamics of what is going on in the unseen spiritual world.

In the KJV it says that "in all this, Job sinned not, nor charged God foolishly." Job was right. God had done nothing to him except remove His protection. Satan was totally responsible for all the evil that occurred to Job, just as he is for all of the evil that occurs to every one of us today. If we break down these Scriptures even further we can see that Satan is the one who influences and is in control of the evil people who come against us:

> And the Sabeans fell upon them, and took them away; yea, they have slain the servants with the edge of the sword; (verse 15) KJV
> While he was yet speaking, there came also another, and said, The Chaldeans made out three bands, and fell upon the camels, and have carried them away, yea, and slain the servants with the edge of the sword; (verse 17) KJV

Yes, it is the Devil, not God who influences evil empires and individuals. It is God who is the one who sets boundaries that the evil ones cannot pass, and prevents them from taking over the entire world.

Neither is God responsible for environmental disasters or deadly weather. There is no such thing as a natural disaster that is an "act of God" as God's accusers are so quick to call them. It is Satan who is behind all of these evil things:

> While he was yet speaking, there came also another, and said "The fire of God is fallen from heaven, and hath burned up the sheep, and the servants, and consumed them;" (verse 16) KJV

> And, behold, there came a great wind from the wilderness, and smote the four corners of the house, and it fell upon the young men, and they are dead; (verse 19) KJV

My dearest friends, listen to the Spirit of God telling you that Satan is the invisible spiritual being who is behind all of these things, even though most of humanity is blind to the truth. They blame human sin on mankind and God. Atheists and Christians alike blame disease and ecological disasters on natural phenomenon, or worse, call them "acts of God", and that's the way Satan wants it. He wants religious people to promote that all evil is the punishment upon humanity from a vengeful, harsh and violent God.

The Devil also wants unbelievers to think that their misfortunes are nothing more than "natural" disasters, evil people and bad luck, with no spiritual component to any of it. Meanwhile, Satan remains concealed, invisibly working behind the scenes to destroy humanity, and nobody is the wiser.

Yes, the Devil wants us to blame God and nature and each other for everything evil in the world, just the way that Adam and Eve did. Yet Satan is the one who is behind it all. As a matter of fact, in a few verses, we will see that Satan is also the one who is behind all infirmity, sickness, and disease as well. But first, let's take a look at how our loving Father in heaven bears the burden of the evil which Satan performs. Even though it was Satan, not God who brought all of this evil into the life of Job, take a look at what God says to Satan:

> Then the Lord asked Satan, "Have you noticed my servant Job? He is the finest man in all the earth. He is blameless—a man of complete integrity. He fears God and stays away from evil. And he has maintained his integrity, even though you urged me to harm him without cause." Job 2:3 NLT

Oh, listen to what the Spirit of God is saying to us here, dear friends. Even though God takes responsibility for all the things that Satan does, we have already seen that it is Satan who performs the evil. He is the one who steals. He is the destroyer. He is the angel of death.

Nonetheless, Satan's power is limited. He must still bow to God and cannot exceed the amount of evil that God permits him to perform. Otherwise, he would have slain Adam and Eve right there in the Garden of Eden before they were ever able to bear any children. Satan could destroy almost all of humanity in a worldwide flood, but He could not touch Noah and His family. He killed many of the children of Israel, but He did not get Moses or Jesus.

Yet, even though Satan has the power of death, we should all thank God that the Scriptures promise us that Christ has conquered Satan's power of death. Speaking of Jesus, the book of Hebrews tells us:

> Because God's children are human beings—made of flesh and blood—the Son also became flesh and blood. For only as a human being could he die, and only by dying could he break the power of the devil, who had the power of death. Hebrews 2: 14 NLT

Now, here we are today in the last generation of mankind before Christ's return and many people are still believing Satan's lies as he blames God for all of the wars, plagues, and ecological disasters in history when, all along, Satan has been the unseen presence causing all of the evil.

Do you think that God is the author of plagues such as Aids and Ebola and Cancer and Covid 19? Do you think that the angel of death who destroyed all of the firstborn in Egypt was one of God's good angels? Look at the next verses in the book of Job with the eyes of your spirit, dear friends, and I pray that you will see that Satan is the invisible evil angel who is behind every infirmity, every sickness, and every disease that has befallen, or ever will befall the human race in the future.

> Satan replied to the Lord, "Skin for skin! A man will give up everything he has to save his life. ⁵ But reach out and take away his health, and he will surely curse you to your face!" "All right, do with him as you please," the Lord said to Satan. "But spare his life." So Satan left the Lord's presence, and he struck Job with terrible boils from head to foot. Job 2:4-6 NLT

I remember as a young child seeing my own father stricken with a few boils on occasion, and let me tell you, they were huge, they were ugly and they were really painful, but when Satan attacked Job with boils, the Scriptures tell us that we are talking about a whole different level of agonizing pain and repulsive physical disfigurement.

From the top of his head to the soles of his feet, Job was completely covered in boils. It was so bad that he couldn't even stand up. He just sat in his pain and lamented of his misery. Even Job's own wife was so overwhelmed with his suffering and disfigurement that she tempted Job to "curse God and die."

> His wife said to him, "Are you still trying to maintain your integrity? Curse God and die." But Job replied, "You talk like a foolish woman. Should we accept only good things from the hand of God and never anything bad?" So in all this, Job said nothing wrong. Job 2: 9-10 NLT

As time goes on, and his friends and relatives abandon and criticize him, Job eventually becomes so depressed with his unrelenting suffering, that he wishes that God would take his life and end it all, yet still Job refuses to deny God.

> "Oh, that I might have my request, that God would grant my desire. I wish he would crush me. I wish he would reach out his hand and kill me. At least I can take comfort in this: Despite the pain, I have not denied the words of the Holy One. But I don't have the strength to endure. I have nothing to live for. Job 6:8-11 NLT

Then the book of Job goes on for another thirty six chapters of Job's friends volunteering varying opinions of why Job is suffering and Job himself complaining and talking to God in speculation of life. Close to the end, Job does make some foolish statements to God in his agony until finally God answers Job. The end result is that God's oration is so magnificent that Job humbles himself before the Lord to repent and admit his own ignorance.

> I take back everything I said, and I sit in dust and ashes to show my repentance." Job 42:6 NLT

Then God in His love and compassion cannot let things go on any longer. He has mercy on Job, putting a stop to Satan's evil and ending Job's suffering. At the same time, God confronts Job's well-meaning but mistaken friends and tells them to now go to Job for prayer so that they do not get what they deserve for accusing Job and misrepresenting God to him (see verses 7-9).

GOD IS OUR DELIVERER, HEALER AND RESTORER

We must never forget that it is SATAN who afflicted Job and GOD who healed and restored him. If Jesus is God manifest in human flesh, the true reflection of Father God in Heaven, the question we need to ask is whether or not God is the giver of diseases or the healer of them? Is Jesus the one who makes humanity suffer and kills us, or is He the one who gives life?

But when Jesus knew it, he withdrew himself from thence: and great multitudes followed him, and he healed them all; Matthew 12:15 KJV

And the whole multitude sought to touch him: for there went virtue out of him, and healed them all. Luke 6:19 KJV

For God so loved the world, that he gave his only begotten Son, that whosoever believeth in him should not perish, but have everlasting life. John 3:16 KJV

So, what happens to Job in the end, the man with the repentant heart? We see that God restores His protection around Job's life. God brings back all of Job's friends and relatives to bless and comfort him, gives him 10 more children, double his original wealth, and another 140 years of life. Job lives so long that he gets to see another four generations of children and grandchildren before he finally dies.

Therefore, listen carefully now. The primary moral of the book of Job is not "everybody must suffer because God is determined to test the faith of us all", as many are teaching today. God does not use evil to test us or tempt us. Satan does.

Let no man say when he is tempted, I am tempted of God: for God cannot be tempted with evil, neither tempteth he any man: James 1:13 KJV

The most important lesson to be learned from the book of Job is that, even though God takes ultimate responsibility for all of the evil which occurs in the world, it is SATAN who is the one who is doing the evil, and this goes all the way back to the Garden of Eden where most people think that God killed Adam and Eve for disobeying Him. Let's read it in Genesis again together, and this time think about everything God has revealed to us in the book of Job:

And the Lord God commanded the man, saying, "Of every tree of the garden thou mayest freely eat: But of the tree of the knowledge of good and evil, thou shalt not eat of it: for in the day that thou eatest thereof thou shalt surely die." Genesis 2:16-17 KJV

Now here is the important question, and I want you to take time to think carefully before you answer. Did God say "If you eat from the tree of knowledge of good and evil, I will kill you"? No! God did not say that! God said "If you eat from the tree of knowledge of good and evil YOU WILL DIE! So, what is the difference?

The difference is that it is Satan who is the one who steals and destroys and kills. In the beginning, as long as Adam and Eve continued to serve and obey God, Satan had no authority or power to afflict them with evil of any kind. At first, Adam and Eve were under God's protection and Satan could not touch them. Sickness could not touch them. Danger could not touch them. Death could not touch them. They even had the opportunity to live forever by eating from the Tree of Life.

It was not until Adam and Eve rejected God's loving authority over them and placed themselves under the dominion of Satan that death came into the picture. Satan lied to Adam and Eve when he told them "You will not die if you trust and obey me" As a matter of fact, if Satan had been honest, this is what he would have told Adam and Eve:

> "If you choose to embrace evil and follow me, I will steal, corrupt and destroy everything that is good in your life. I will even bring harm to the wonderful biological body that God has given you. It will become diseased and frail and dried out until it can no longer function and finally crumbles back into the dust from which it came. Yes, if you follow me, in the end I WILL EVENTUALLY KILL YOU and then my demons will take you to hell"

You see, dear friends, it was sin and Satan, not God who killed Adam and his wife Eve after they chose to embrace evil. The Bible does not tell us when Eve died, but we know she lived long enough to bear many children and the Word of God does tell us that God was the One who gave Adam well over another 900 years of health and life so he could see his children and grandchildren grow up for many generations before God reluctantly and finally allowed Satan to take Adam's life.

EVIL BEGINS TO CORRUPT HUMANITY

Now, let's go back to Genesis and take a look at a couple of other evils of life that God has long been blamed for, and yet the truth is that Satan is the real guilty party, the one who is behind all of man's suffering:

> Unto the woman he said, I will greatly multiply thy sorrow and thy conception; in sorrow thou shalt bring forth children; and thy desire shall be to thy husband, and he shall rule over thee. Genesis 3:16 KJV

Dear friends, don't listen to anyone who tells you that infertility or pain in childbirth is God pronouncing punishment on women for Eve's disobedience, or that God ordains that men are superior to women and can treat women any way they want. These types of statements are nothing more than Satan again speaking through people to try to accuse God for all of the evil that he himself does.

Yes, God says here in Genesis "I will do this", but after we take these statements in the context of the revelation that we already know from what God has given us in the book of Job, it is important that we realize that God is saying that (because of the presence of evil) it will happen and "I am taking responsibility for this", but Satan is always the one who is always performing the evil.

Many people today do not know God's goodness or His loving nature, so they argue: "Why would a good and loving God ever allow evil to happen?" They say they refuse to believe and follow a God who permits so much evil to occur in the world and does nothing about it. Furthermore, there are many professing Christians who are unfortunately just as confused as the unbelievers are on this topic. Whenever something goes wrong in their lives, they keep blaming God for the Devil's actions (or their own folly-for that matter).

I have heard Christians preach and teach that evil has to exist. They suggest that there has to be evil in the world in order for us to understand

and appreciate the goodness of God. They speak of God testing and teaching mankind through the things which we suffer as the result of evil in the world. They talk about Adam and Eve as being "innocent" before the fall, which is a true statement.

However, these preachers mistakenly teach that this means that Adam and Eve were incapable of discerning the difference between good and evil until they made the choice to reject God and embrace evil.

No! No! No! That is not at all true! I expose your deception Satan. Let the truth be known by the Spirit of God in the name of Jesus. Adam and Eve were innocent, but they were not stupid. They were not incapable of intellectually discerning the difference between good and evil. In fact, without presence of evil to hinder and corrupt their intelligence, they were probably a lot smarter than anyone here on Earth today.

THERE ARE TWO KINDS OF KNOWLEDGE

Those who say that evil had to come into our world and has to continue to exist are still stuck in the unscriptural mindset that God is the one who materializes physical evil into the world. They have not even considered that there are actually two ways for us to "know" evil.

First there is the intellectual or "discerning" way to know evil. This is the knowledge of evil that comes through the knowledge of good combined with trust and faith in God. It comes from following God's goodness. In this kind of knowledge, there is no harm, pain, sorrow or death.

Then there is the "experiential" way to know evil. That kind of knowledge comes from participating in evil, experiencing evil first-hand. It comes from thinking and speaking and behaving wickedly, and making evil part of our nature, including evil as part of our daily behavior.

Jesus Christ is our living testimony that it is possible for a totally sinless human being to have the ability to intellectually and spiritually "discern" between good and evil without actually participating in evil and making evil part of our nature.

These people who say that evil has to exist in our world are wrong. The tree of knowledge of good and evil did not represent the ability to comprehend or discern the difference between good and evil. Adam and

Eve already inherently had that intellectual and spiritual ability because God created man to be "very good" in nature, just like God Himself.

As long as Adam and Eve continued to trust and obey God, by FAITH they would always be able to intellectually know and discern the difference between good and evil and they would never have to suffer through "knowing" evil by EXPERIENCE.

Even the Hebrew word for "know" used in Genesis in reference to the knowledge of good and evil is the very same word that is used when God says that Adam "knew" his wife and she conceived and bore a son.

The word implies that the tree of knowledge of good and evil represented a desire to experience an intimate personal relationship with evil. This type of knowledge of evil is the type of knowledge which comes only from experiencing and practicing evil.

Let me give you an example of what I am talking about. When a loving parent sees their young child getting too close to a hot stove burner, we tell our children. No! That is hot! It will hurt you! Now the child is faced with a decision. If they trust and have faith in their parents and obey them, they can continue the rest of their life in the safety of having the "intellectual" or "discerning" knowledge that the activated stove element is hot.

We can absolutely "know" through faith and trust in the words and integrity of our parents that we must not touch the hot stove element with our bare skin or it will harm us. We can also know by believing our parents that we need to be extra careful whenever we are around a hot stove, because even if we touch it by accident, we could be seriously harmed.

Yet how many of us as children just had to learn that knowledge by experience. We decided that we just had to touch that hot stove, or were careless around the stove and fell against it, or knocked something hot on ourselves. Then we "knew" from painful experience what we could have known from trust and faith and obedience, if we had only listened to and obeyed our parents in the first place.

No, Adam and Eve were innocent in the beginning, but they were not stupid. They were not incapable of comprehending and rejecting evil. Their choice to eat from the tree was an expression of their desire to experience evil, to participate in it, just as mankind still wants to participate in evil to this very day.

CHAPTER 9

Evil Begins to Spread

INFERTILITY AND PAIN IN CHILDBIRTH

If you remember, we discerned from Genesis that, in order for Adam and Eve to "know" or intimately experience evil, God's glory first had to depart so that darkness could come into Adam and Eve's lives. The light had to leave so the darkness could come in.

Furthermore, we need to understand the true gravity of the situation here. If God had permitted it, Satan would have killed Adam and Eve immediately, right then and there on same the day that they chose to reject God and put themselves under Satan's dominion of evil. That way, Satan could have thwarted any possibility of man's Redeemer being born. Certainly, this was Satan's original plan, but God spoiled the Devil's scheme by refusing to allow Satan to kill Adam and Eve right away.

Do not forget that even though Satan is the angel who has the power of death, God still has control over when Satan is allowed to exercise that power. If not for God, Satan would have taken Adam and Eve's lives before they ever had the opportunity to bear any children. However, Satan did not have the authority or power to do that. God had already decreed before they disobeyed that man and woman were to go forth and multiply (Genesis 1:28).

Since we know that (in the beginning) everything God created was very good, we can say with Scriptural support that women experiencing pain in childbirth was never in the perfect will of God. In fact, it was never God's will for mankind to ever experience any pain at all. Rather, Revelation 21:4 tells us that pain will be one of the things that will cease to exist in human experience once the Devil is finally cast into the Lake of Fire.

You see, the situation in the Garden of Eden was that Satan knew he did not have God's permission to take Adam and Eve's lives right away. So Satan's alternate goal was to try to prevent and discourage childbirth through infertility and pain. However, never forget that (even though Adam and Eve chose to place humanity under Satan's dominion) God has always had the authority to limit the extent of the evil that the Devil can perform, and God is also loving, merciful and forgiving.

Satan was not permitted to immediately kill Adam and Eve or stop them from bearing children, but he was allowed by God to interfere with fertility, and bring pain and discomfort into the experience of childbirth. Satan's obvious goal was that (through pain) this would discourage women from wanting to have any children, (fear of pain), or wanting to have more than one child (memory of pain). However, God countered that move by giving Eve such overwhelming joy in seeing her children born that it greatly outweighed the pain she had to suffer during pregnancy in order to bear her children.

> A woman when she is in travail hath sorrow, because her hour is come: but as soon as she is delivered of the child, she remembereth no more the anguish, for joy that a man is born into the world. John 16:21 KJV

Then after Eve's first child (Cain) is born, Satan immediately goes to work on tempting Cain to reject God and follow the ways of evil, with the intent of influencing Cain to murder his whole family, starting with his younger brother Abel. But once again, God limits the evil Satan can do. After his brother's murder, God exiles Cain from his immediate family and sends him out from their presence before he can harm anyone else.

EVIL SPREADS TO ALL OF MAN'S DOMINION

In Genesis, the Lord tells us that after creation was completed, God surveyed all that He had made and proclaimed all of it to be "very good". It is important for us to understand that the consequence of Adam's decision to reject God and embrace evil is that man's "very good" dominion then became part of (and subject to) Satan's "very evil" dominion.

This meant that Satan was going to do his best to corrupt and destroy everything that God had created. Everything that is very good, Satan hates and wants to corrupt and destroy. God also reminds Adam in Genesis 3 that he did not evolve from anything. He was made by God from the very dust of the ground he was standing on.

> And to the man he said, Since you listened to your wife and ate from the tree whose fruit I commanded you not to eat, the ground is cursed because of you. All your life you will struggle to scratch a living from it. It will grow thorns and thistles for you, though you will eat of its grains. By the sweat of your brow will you have food to eat until you return to the ground from which you were made, for you were made from dust, and to dust you will return." Genesis 3:17-19 NLT

Later on in Genesis 5, a man named Lamech, the father of Noah would declare that the Lord has cursed the ground. Yet, that is not what the Scripture says here. God says that the ground is cursed because of Adam's actions. Actually, it is Satan who is the one who right away began making life difficult for Adam and Eve (and all mankind) by making the ground infertile and hard to till, and filling it with weeds and thorns to try to turn mankind against God. Then, throughout our lives and right up to the very end, it is also Satan who brings sickness, infirmity and death to all of us.

God's Word tells us that Death is actually God's ENEMY and will be the last enemy to be defeated before God creates the new heavens and Earth. In fact, we are told that when the new Earth is created after the Millennium, God's will shall finally be completely done on Earth as it is in Heaven. Satan will be gone permanently, and from that day forward there will never again be any pain, sorrow, sickness or death in all of God's Kingdom forever.

> The last enemy that shall be destroyed is death. 1 Corinthians 15:26 KJV
>
> And death and hell were cast into the lake of fire. This is the second death. Revelation 20:14 KJV
>
> And God shall wipe away all tears from their eyes; and there shall be no more death, neither sorrow, nor crying, neither shall there be any more pain: for the former things are passed away. Revelation 21:4 KJV

SATAN'S CORRUPTION EXTENDS INTO OUTER SPACE

You may not have thought much about this before now, but in the beginning, God's desire and plan for mankind went far beyond the planet we now live on. With no infertility, no pain in childbirth and the ability to bear children for many centuries, if there was no evil to hinder mankind, human reproduction would have filled the Earth to capacity in a very short time, perhaps as little as a couple of thousand years. Then what?

The reality of our present situation is that, through our own puny intellectual and technological efforts, man is nearing the goal of being able to colonize the moon and possibly other planets as well if mankind does not self-destruct before we reach that stage. Is it not logical then that it was God's will all along for man to eventually expand out into the universe around us, all of which, remember, was created for mankind's benefit in the first place?

However, the material universe which now exists is nothing like the universe which God originally created. Just like on Earth, Satan has been corrupting the moon, planets and stars for thousands of years to the point that the Scriptures tell us that God is going to have to create it all anew at the end of the Millennium.

As we are now about to examine in the Bible, Satan's corruption of the heavens actually played a very prominent role in the destruction of the Earth during the flood of Noah's day. But before we get into that, I think that it is important for us to examine what the Bible has to say about Satan being directly involved in the world's first examples of false religion and the world's first murder involving a man killing another man.

THERE IS NO SALVATION IN FALSE RELIGION

We already discussed in a previous chapter that when Adam and Eve sinned, their covering of God's Glory departed from them. As soon as that happened, the first knowledge of evil that Satan imparted to Adam and Eve was that they were now naked and they needed to hide or cover their sin. The Devil filled them full of shame and impressed upon them that they should cover their nakedness. Then Satan filled them with fear and condemnation, and convinced them that they needed to hide from the Lord. So man became afraid of God.

> At that moment their eyes were opened, and they suddenly felt shame at their nakedness. So they sewed fig leaves together to cover themselves. When the cool evening breezes were blowing, the man and his wife heard the Lord God walking about in the garden. So they hid from the Lord God among the trees. Then the Lord God called to the man, "Where are you?" He replied, "I heard you walking in the garden, so I hid. I was afraid because I was naked." "Who told you that you were naked?" the Lord God asked... Genesis 3:7-11 NLT

Indeed, God would not have asked them this question if there was not an answer. "Who told you that you were naked?" It was Satan who had told them they were naked. Satan had filled them with shame and condemnation. Satan had filled them with fear of God and fear of death, and as we discussed earlier, Satan also filled them with the desire to deceive, and they tried to blame the serpent, each other and God for what they had done.

DEATH ENTERS THE FALLEN WORLD

Actually, the first deaths on Earth were not people. They were animals. The Word of God does not specifically elaborate on exactly how the first animals on Earth died. Some have suggested that God killed and skinned them to impress upon man the horribleness of our sin. I am not denying that such a thing could have happened, but there is no real Biblical support for it occurring and I believe it is out of character for God to do such a thing.

When we remember that it is Satan, not God, who is the bringer of death, I think that it is far more likely that, in order to add to Adam and Eve's sorrow and fear of God, as soon as Adam and Eve sinned, Satan began to cause some of the animals to drop dead right in front of Adam and Eve. Satan could not kill Adam and Eve right away, but he could strike fear in their hearts by killing animals. But instead of punishing and condemning Adam and Eve, God had compassion on them.

I believe that God explained to them that it was their sin that was responsible for this, and their sin could not be covered by their own bloodless works. Instead, God took away their false fig leaf religion and the Lord made skins from some of the animals who had died.

God explained to Adam and Eve that they needed to clothe themselves with those animal skins as a reminder that they were responsible for bringing evil and death into the world. I believe that God told them that if they repented of evil and obeyed the Lord, God would accept their wearing of these skins as a covering for man's sin until mankind's Redeemer came.

Of course, since there was not always going to be a freshly dead animal around every time they needed clothing for their growing families, mankind would soon find out that if they were going to continue to be obedient to God, they would have to suffer the heartrendingly unpleasant task of slaying animals themselves in order to obtain the animal skins to make new clothing for their growing families. It would be just another reminder to mankind that Satan and humanity, not God, are responsible for bringing sin and death into the world.

Furthermore, this was a ritual that man was expected to continue to honor and practice until the Redeemer came. Once you realize this, it gives a whole new significance to the fact that John the Baptist chose camel's hair and an animal skin for his clothing. John still honored God's command to Adam and Eve.

Yet, all of that ended with John the Baptist. Ever since Christ became God's sacrificial lamb, we are now covered and redeemed by the blood of Jesus Christ and clothed with His righteousness. Now we partake of communion in remembrance of that and are free to modestly wear whatever we want, but before Christ died and rose again, John the Baptist demonstrated that he still understood and honored God's way of redemption and covering man's sins. Thus, John wore animal skin and preached repentance.

MANKIND'S FIRST CHILDREN

Let's now take another look at Adam and Eve's first children. For Eve, childbirth did not happen right away because of Satan's ability to hinder fertility, but over time, Eve gave birth to two sons. The older, who became a farmer, was named Cain. The younger, who became a shepherd, was called Abel.

> Now Adam had sexual relations with his wife, Eve, and she became pregnant. When she gave birth to Cain, she said, "With the Lord's help, I have produced a man!" Later she gave birth to his brother and named him Abel. When they grew up, Abel became a shepherd, while Cain cultivated the ground. Genesis 4:1-2 NLT

The first thing to note here is Eve's acknowledgement of the necessity of God's participation in enabling her to conceive and bear children. In the KJV, we see that Eve does not even say that the child is "hers", but acknowledges that "I have gotten a man from the Lord." (Genesis 4:1 KJV). I think that this is one of a couple of indicators that (in spite of being responsible for humanity's fall) we may see Adam and Eve in heaven. What a difference that is between the wicked attitude of today that "the child is mine and I have the right to abort it if I want to."

As for Adam and Eve, they repented and wore the skins that God gave them. They were grateful to God for their children and taught their children to worship God.

The Bible does not tell us a lot about Abel, but there are a few very important details about him in the Word of God if you know where to look for them. First, the book of Luke lists Abel as one of God's prophets:

> Therefore also said the wisdom of God, I will send them prophets and apostles, and some of them they shall slay and persecute: That the blood of all the prophets, which was shed from the foundation of the world, may be required of this generation; From the blood of Abel unto the blood of Zacharias which perished between the altar and the temple: verily I say unto you, It shall be required of this generation. Luke 11: 49-51 KJV

The book of Hebrews also speaks of Abel, testifying that He was a righteous man, a man of faith in God, a man who was determined to walk in obedience to God.

> It was by faith that Abel brought a more acceptable offering to God than Cain did. Abel's offering gave evidence that he was a righteous man, and God showed his approval of his gifts. Although Abel is long dead, he still speaks to us by his example of faith. Hebrews 11:4 NLT

THERE IS NO SALVATION IN DEAD WORKS

Let's now take a look at the Genesis record of Cain and Abel, and how the two men differed according to the Word of God. We already know that God declared Abel was a righteous man of faith and obedience, and that he was a prophet. Now, let's go back to Genesis now and see how the story of Cain and Abel unfolds.

> When it was time for the harvest, Cain presented
> some of his crops as a gift to the Lord. Abel also brought
> a gift—the best portions of the firstborn lambs from his
> flock. The Lord accepted Abel and his gift, but he did not
> accept Cain and his gift. This made Cain very angry, and
> he looked dejected. Genesis 4:3-5 NLT

Some have tried to use this passage to suggest that the raising of livestock is a higher and more honorable occupation than farming, but that is simply not true. Cain chose the same profession as his father Adam and it was a perfectly honorable way to earn a living, growing the food to feed your family and the community.

We must remember that this was back in the time when God had not instructed man to kill animals for food. Some may have eaten meat before the flood, but God had only authorized man to eat a vegetarian diet. So Cain provided a very important service for human society.

> Then God said, "Look! I have given you every seed-
> bearing plant throughout the earth and all the fruit trees
> for your food. And I have given every green plant as food
> for all the wild animals, the birds in the sky, and the
> small animals that scurry along the ground—everything
> that has life." And that is what happened. Genesis 1:29-
> 30 NLT

The same thing could be said about Abel. Abel knew that the world would need a steady supply of animal skins for clothing if humanity was going to continue to obey God, so he chose to make it his profession to raise livestock to provide clothing for his family, and sell or trade his livestock to others as they had need for their families, and he probably would have marketed milk as well. At this point in history, the rest of the skinned animal may have been simply discarded or burned as an offering to God. We don't really know because the Bible does not go into detail about it.

Well, then. What was the difference between the two men? They both had honorable professions. They both freely brought an offering to

God without God asking for it, so why did God honor Abel's offering and reject Cain's? You don't really need to go very far to get the answer to that question, and it had nothing to do with Cain's occupation as a farmer or that there was anything wrong with his offering to God from his harvest.

> We must not be like Cain, who belonged to the evil one
> and killed his brother. And why did he kill him? Because
> Cain had been doing what was evil, and his brother had
> been doing what was righteous. 1 John 3:12 NLT

You see, dear friends, as John shows us here, the problem was not that there was anything wrong with the content of Cain's offering. The problem was that Cain was a sinful and unrepentant man, and in his own vanity, Cain thought that he could offer his gift to God in restitution for his continuing evil ways.

People do exactly the same thing in our generation. Wicked people go on Santa's toy runs, or make big donations to secular charities, or pay tithes, or do religious service. Some of them even stand in pulpits and preach, believing that this will excuse them before God for all of their other wickedness and unrepentance. But God says, we must not be like Cain.

Listen carefully, because this is what God had to say to Cain, and to every other person on Earth who thinks that they are going to get away with continuing to disobey the Lord just because we also do charitable works, or do religious works, or claim to be a Christian:

> "Why are you so angry?" the Lord asked Cain. "Why
> do you look so dejected? You will be accepted if you do
> what is right. But if you refuse to do what is right, then
> watch out! Sin is crouching at the door, eager to control
> you. But you must subdue it and be its master."
> Genesis 4:6-7 NLT

Here is the real root of the problem. Cain was angry and upset that God would not accept his offering, but when God confronts Cain about his unrepentance, he does not change his ways. He becomes even more angry and violent.

In addition to this, I can also almost guarantee you that God is not the only one who spoke to Cain about his evil ways. If you remember, God told us that Abel was a prophet in Luke, and let me tell you this. If you know anything about prophets, you will understand that they do not keep God's word to themselves. The Word of God burns like a fire within them, and their love for humanity is such that they are going to speak the Word of God to others (regardless of the consequences) in hope that people will repent and be saved.

There is no doubt at all in my mind that Abel tried to encourage his brother to change his ways, repent, and walk in obedience to God, and that is probably what cost him his life in the end, because God says:

> One day Cain suggested to his brother, "Let's go out into the fields." And while they were in the field, Cain attacked his brother, Abel, and killed him. Genesis 4:8 NLT

So Cain rejected God, refused to repent, followed the ways of Satan and how did that work out for him? He ended up killing his own brother and God exiled Cain from his family so he could do no more harm. Then, after God removed his protective blessing from Cain because he refused to abandon his evil ways, did Satan reward him for following him? No! Cain had started out as a successful farmer, but once he departed from God to keep following the Devil, the guy was not even able to farm any more. Satan saw to it that the ground would no longer yield a harvest for Cain.

No matter how hard Cain worked, Satan ensured that his crops did not grow. Cain ended up a homeless vagabond wandering far from God and fearful that someone else would kill him for the evil he had done. That is the kind of reward Satan will give you for serving him with your life. It reminds me of what happens to many drug addicts. Follow the Devil, and he will promise you paradise, but give you sickness, poverty and death in the end.

Yet, even in God's banishment, God was merciful. God placed a mark on Cain, not as a punishment, but as a warning to anyone who got it in their head that they would be doing service to God if they killed Cain. As horrendous as Cain's crime was, God's mark was a symbol of God's mercy and love for Cain, not punishment.

Yes, it was a reminder to Cain of what he had done, but also a warning to others that they were not permitted to kill Cain, and it was an opportunity for Cain to repent and start over, even though there is no indication in Scripture that Cain ever changed his evil ways.

> Cain replied to the Lord, "My punishment is too great for me to bear! You have banished me from the land and from your presence; you have made me a homeless wanderer. Anyone who finds me will kill me!" The Lord replied, "No, for I will give a sevenfold punishment to anyone who kills you." Then the Lord put a mark on Cain to warn anyone who might try to kill him. So Cain left the Lord's presence and settled in the land of Nod, east of Eden. Genesis 4:13-16 NLT

Take note of Cain's attitude in all of this. He still doesn't acknowledge his sin. He still does not repent. First he blames God for his plight and then takes it on himself to depart completely from God's presence and dwell in the land of Nod. In Hebrew, the word "nod" means "vagrancy-wandering-exile".

Then the Bible tells us that Lamech, one of Cain's descendants becomes the world's second murderer. Lamech had the audacity to take it upon himself to declare that he was also under God's protection from retribution for His murderous crime, even though God had said no such thing.

Evil was certainly progressing rapidly throughout the human race. However, as we continue to study God's Word, we learn that not all of mankind were evil before the flood. There were still a few who loved God and refused to follow Satan.

CHAPTER 10

God Covered Man's Sin

THERE WERE BELIEVERS ON EARTH BEFORE THE FLOOD.

As already mentioned, it appears from Scripture that Adam and Eve repented of their sin after the fall of man, and Abel is certainly honored by God as a believer, but the Scriptures suggest that in the beginning, there may also have been numerous other people who returned to God before the flood, and the first of these was Adam's third son Seth, followed by Seth's son Enos, and although they are not named, Genesis 4:26 implies that there were others as well.

> And Adam knew his wife again; and she bare a son, and called his name Seth: For God, said she, hath appointed me another seed instead of Abel, whom Cain slew. And to Seth, to him also there was born a son; and he called his name Enos: then began men to call upon the name of the Lord. Genesis 4:25-26 KJV

Another reason to consider Seth and Enos as believers is that they are listed in Christ's lineage, as given in Luke 3:38. After this (other than recording the lineage of believers), the Bible does not have anything more to say about the degeneration of human society until about 450 years later when a man named "Enoch" comes on the scene.

Once again, this is another example where not much is said about Enoch in Genesis, but if we go to Hebrews, we can learn that Enoch was a man of faith who pleased God, so much so that God took him up to heaven without even dying. Enoch's disappearance was actually a type or shadow of Jesus coming for His Bride of believers to remove us in the near future from this present wicked and rebellious generation of humanity who have not much desire at all to please God, just as it was in the days of Noah.

> By faith Enoch was translated that he should not see death; and was not found, because God had translated him: for before his translation he had this testimony, that he pleased God. Hebrews 11:5 KJV

In addition, the book of Jude tells us that Enoch was a man who prophesied of coming judgement upon unrepentant people, and of a later time when the Lord will return to Earth with a multitude of His saints.

Evidence of Enoch's prophetic anointing is further reinforced when we realize that at age 65 Enoch named his first son "Methuselah" which means in Hebrew "when he dies, it (the judgement of God) will come."

> And Enoch also, the seventh from Adam, prophesied of these, saying, Behold, the Lord cometh with ten thousands of his saints, Jude 14 KJV

> When Enoch was 65 years old, he became the father of Methuselah. After the birth of Methuselah, Enoch lived in close fellowship with God for another 300 years, and he had other sons and daughters. Enoch lived 365 years, walking in close fellowship with God. Then one day he disappeared, because God took him. Genesis 5:21-24 NLT

Now, some people know that the Bible records Methuselah as being the world's oldest man, living to the ripe old age of nine hundred and sixty-nine years before dying. Although there are some who question the truth of Methuselah's age, I do not doubt it for a moment because I believe that God said it and every word of God is true, and for me, that settles it.

I also believe from the Word of God that it was God's long-suffering and mercy and desire to give humanity every opportunity to repent that was the reason Methuselah came to be the world's oldest man. In case anyone is interested, the Bible also records Jared (Methuselah's grandfather) and Noah as being the next two oldest people at 962 years and 950 years. Yes, yes, yes! It's true. They actually lived that long, you doubters. Stop doubting the Word of God.

There are also a couple of other things to take note of about the life of Methuselah. He too is mentioned in the lineage of Jesus Christ in Chapter 3 of the book of Luke, and from there you can see that Methuselah was actually Noah's grandfather so the writers of the New Testament also believed what Moses had to say about Methuselah and his age in Genesis, even if some people today do not.

Then if you go back to Genesis 5 and do the math, you will find that Methuselah was still alive when Noah was building the Ark. As a matter of fact, God's Word tells us that Methuselah died the same year that the flood destroyed the world, just as Enoch had prophesied would happen. Do you remember that Methuselah's name meant "when he dies, it will come"?

So the idea of a cruel and heartless God suddenly bringing a flood down and destroying all of humanity without giving mankind any warning, or mercy, or chance to be saved is a horrible misrepresentation of God, and of what actually happened, and of who it really was who brought the flood upon humanity and destroyed the original creation of God.

According to Genesis 5, we know that Enoch was 65 years old when Methuselah was born, so God gave humanity at least 969 years to repent by extending Methuselah's lifespan to make him the longest living man in human history because:

> ...God waited patiently while Noah was building his
> boat. Only eight people were saved from drowning in that
> terrible flood. 1 Peter 3: 20 NLT

You see, not only did humanity have the 969 years of Methuselah's lifespan to repent, mankind was given several other clear "signs" from God that judgement was coming. It would have taken years for Noah and his family to build an Ark of salvation as large as the Bible says it was. The Ark was 450 feet long by 75 feet wide and 45 feet high. This is longer than a football field. It was about the same length as some modern freighters and about one third the size of a modern cruise ship.

Yet during all of the time Noah was building the Ark, (and undoubtedly preaching about God's coming judgement) human society mocked him and degenerated into worse and worse wickedness. Even when Methuselah died, there was probably some terror in the beginning as the human race waited to see what would happen next. Yet when nothing bad immediately occurred, humanity still refused to repent of their evil ways.

The Ark easily had the capacity to house all of the animals and many hundreds of people, but no one believed God's prophets. During the last year before the flood, they ignored the increasingly urgent warnings of Noah, and grew even more evil than they were before, until there was no good left in them (see Genesis 5:5)

What does it take for God to convince man to turn away from evil? The wicked of humanity always want another "sign" from God before they will repent, but even when God sent the miracle of mated pairs of all the animals on Earth coming right up to Noah and marching peacefully into the Ark two by two, mankind still refused to acknowledge that this was a sign from God that they should repent and follow them into the Ark.

Why did they not repent? Because the Word of God tells us that all of the remainder of humanity had become so consumed by evil that they were even allowing demons to possess them, producing genetic corruption in their children which resulted in human giants being born who were very evil:

> And it came to pass, when men began to multiply on the face of the earth, and daughters were born unto them, that the sons of God saw the daughters of men that they were fair; and they took them wives of all which they chose. Genesis 6:1-2 KJV

There are three main variations of opinion among Bible scholars as to what this passage means. Some suggest that the "sons of God" refers to believers fornicating with beautiful, but unsaved (and probably demon-possessed) women creating genetically corrupt offspring. Others have the opinion that there were evil angels who took on a physical form and had sex with human women, and the giants were the result of these unions.

I do not think that either of these are accurate representations of this Scripture. For one thing, if these sons of God were true believers, they would not be going around having sex with unsaved demon possessed women, no matter how beautiful they were.

Secondly, God's Word indicates that the angels are a different "kind" of lifeform than human beings and they do not in themselves have the ability to reproduce, not even among their own kind (see Mark 12:25). That is why God created an uncountable number of angels all at once. They do not reproduce.

The train of thought on this Scripture which makes the most sense to me has a link to what we have already examined in the book of Job. There we discovered that even though the angels are not God's offspring created in the image and likeness of God as we are, the Lord still refers to them as created sons of God. There is also one place in the book of Job where God confronts Job by basically saying "You think that you know everything, but where were you when I laid the foundations of the Earth during creation:

> Where wast thou when I laid the foundations of the earth? Declare, if thou hast understanding... When the morning stars sang together, and all the sons of God shouted for joy? Job 38:4-7 KJV

This Scripture would indicate that, before man came along, there were angelic beings in heaven whom the Lord referred to as sons of God who rejoiced during the creation of the Earth, and these were the same angels who were still reporting their activities to God when Satan came with them to report his own activities and complain to God about Job many centuries later:

> Now there was a day when the sons of God came to present themselves before the Lord, and Satan came also among them. Job 1:6 KJV

I believe that there is one other important point to make here. Even though angels are commonly portrayed in human artworks in female and baby form, as well as males, there is nothing in Scripture to support this idea. In the Bible, angels are always referred to as being in male form, and it is somewhat obvious that the concept of female and baby angels actually arises from the unbiblical religious teachings that human beings become angels when they die. We do not!

Angels are distinctly different "kind" of being from human beings, just as human beings are different "kind" of being from all other life on Earth. We are the only "kind" of being created in God's own image and after God's own likeness, and only reproduce after our own kind.

In this context then, I believe that what was happening before the flood was that evil angelic beings (who had started their existence as the angelic "sons of God" became infatuated with the beauty of human women and many of them were taking possession of wicked human men in order that (through these men) those angels could participate in the lustful experience of sex with human women while further corrupting the human race.

These unholy unions resulted in human genetic corruption of all kinds, and one of the side effects of this evil behavior was that sometimes the offspring of the demon-possessed grew to be powerful giants. In fact, this kind of behavior even resumed to some degree after the flood amongst the heathen, resulting in the birth of Goliath (whom David slew) and other evil giants amongst the Philistines and other wicked nations of the world.

> There were giants in the earth in those days; and also after that, when the sons of God came in unto the daughters of men, and they bare children to them, the same became mighty men which were of old, men of renown. Genesis 6:4 KJV

I believe that this perception of what happened is also supported elsewhere in Scripture where God declares that angels who left their realm and their created form and possessed human beings to entice mankind toward sexual debauchery are paying for their evil by being kept in everlasting chains of darkness until the judgement day:

> And the angels which kept not their first estate, but left their own habitation, he hath reserved in everlasting

chains under darkness unto the judgment of the great day.
Jude v. 6 KJV

The implication in Genesis 5 is that, as bad as Sodom and Gomorrah was for violence and sexual sin, the state of humanity before the flood was just as bad, because God declared that (with the exception of Noah and his family) by the time of the flood, every thought of mankind had become evil continuously. Like their master Satan whom they all followed, there was no longer any good in them:

> And God saw that the wickedness of man was great
> in the earth, and that every imagination of the thoughts
> of his heart was only evil continually. Genesis 6:5 KJV

The situation had become so bad that God declared mankind would no longer be permitted to have such a long life span (because the longer they lived, the more evil they became). God decreed that man's new life span would be limited to one hundred and twenty years (Genesis 6:3), and within a few short generations after the flood, that prophecy of God had come true.

If you follow the record of Genesis, you will see that after the flood, Noah died at age 950. Noah lived almost as long as Methuselah, but his son Shem only reached an age of 600 years and then he died.

Shem's sons and grandsons died before they reached 500 years and their descendants never reached 300 years. This was probably when Job lived, because the Bible indicates that Job was probably still fathering children when he was well into his 200's (living another 150 years after his first ten children died).

By the time we Get to Abraham's father Terah, who died at age 205, and Abraham who died at age 175, these men were considered to be exceptionally old, and only a couple of generations later we find that Moses, the most godly man of his generation died at age 120, and that's been pretty close to the maximum survivable age for humanity ever since then, with the average human lifespan being much less than that. Moses observed in Psalm 90:10 that man's average life span was around seventy years, and that is where it remains to this day.

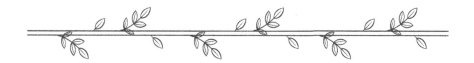

CHAPTER 11

Who Builds and Who Destroys?

WHO DESTROYED THE WORLD WITH A FLOOD?

The unfortunate reality is that no matter what I say and what the Word of God says, there will be people who will read the Genesis account of the flood and argue that God destroyed all of mankind in the flood, including innocent women and children.

They will point to Genesis 6 (ignoring the part that says the world was filled with violence and every thought of man's heart was evil continually) and they'll say "See-the Christian Bible says your God destroyed innocent women and children!"

> And God said unto Noah, The end of all flesh is come before me; for the earth is filled with violence through them; and, behold, I will destroy them with the earth. Genesis 6:13 KJV

With feigned indignation, they will say that they could never worship a God who would condemn Adam and Eve to death for an innocent act of disobedience like eating a piece of fruit. They will ask you what kind of cruel and vengeful God would destroy all life on Earth (even children and babies) via a worldwide flood.

These are the same people who say they refuse to believe in a God who would send homosexuals and prostitutes and adulterers and those who abort their children, and ALL sinners to an eternal fiery hell. Yet their objections do not come from a heart of love. They say these things because they are accusers of God, just like their father, the Devil.

Those who believe and teach these things are willingly ignorant that God did not want Adam and Eve to die and strongly warned them not to embrace evil. They are willingly ignorant that God "covered" Adam and Eve's sin for many centuries before reluctantly allowing Satan to take their lives.

They are willingly ignorant that God warned mankind to repent for many centuries before the flood and declared that by the time of the flood (with the exception of Noah and his immediate family) there was no one left living on the Earth whose every thought in their heads was not evil continually.

We see exactly the same thing happening in these corrupt end times we now live in. The world without God is becoming ever more wicked by the day. They are themselves heartless and lawless and violent, and yet they accuse the Bible and belief in God of being the cause for humanity's woes, making no distinction between real Christianity and all of the false religion of the world, (including false Christianity).

People invent vain theories of evolution and billion year gaps between the creation of Earth and the creation of man. They are willingly ignorant that the Earth was created before the sun, moon and stars and deny that there ever was a worldwide flood. They mock the Word of God, saying there is no hell and say Christ is not coming again for the repentant who love Him, and they keep on sinning, repeatedly demanding a sign from God before they will believe God and repent.

This is my second letter to you, dear friends, and in both of them I have tried to stimulate your wholesome thinking and refresh your memory. I want you to remember what the holy prophets said long ago and what our Lord and Savior commanded through your apostles. Most importantly, I want to remind you that in the last days, scoffers will come, mocking the truth and following their own desires. They will say, "What happened to the promise that Jesus is coming again? From before the times of our ancestors, everything has remained the same since the world was first created." They deliberately forget that God made the heavens long ago by the word of his command, and he brought the earth out from the water and surrounded it with water. Then he used the water to destroy the ancient world with a mighty flood. And by the same word, the present heavens and earth have been stored up for fire. They are being kept for the Day of Judgment, when ungodly people will be destroyed. 2 Peter 3:1-7 NLT

Yes, those who accuse God are willingly ignorant that God does not want anyone to die in the Tribulation. They are willingly ignorant that God warned mankind to repent of evil and come back to Him for over a thousand years before finally withdrawing His protection to allow SATAN to destroy the world with a flood. That's right! I said that it was not God who destroyed those who followed the Devil. It was Satan who destroyed his own followers and the world with a worldwide flood in Noah's day.

IS GOD OUR KILLER?

I ask you this question. Does God want to destroy anyone? God is the One who loves mankind! He wants us to live! He wants us to come back to Him.

The Lord isn't really being slow about his promise, as some people think. No, he is being patient for your sake. He does not want anyone to be destroyed, but wants everyone to repent. 2 Peter 3:9 NLT

God was the One who had Noah build an Ark for mankind's salvation. God is the one who is merciful. Regardless of how much wickedness they had done throughout their entire lives, all mankind had to do was repent of their sins, believe Noah and God, and get into the Ark to be saved. Yet, they would not do it, because their hearts and deeds were evil, just like the Devil, the one that they had chosen to serve as their father.

I urge you to stop believing that it is God who kills people. That is the work of Satan, the accuser. Do you remember the pattern laid out for us in the book of Job? Even though God bears the burden for all evil, God is the One who creates and blesses and protects and restores. Satan is the one who curses and steals and destroys and kills. He is the one who has the power of death over humanity.

Even though it grieved God greatly to do so, at the appointed time, the Lord finally closed the door of the Ark to protect everyone who believed in Him. Then the Ark took them up above the flood that Satan brought upon humanity to kill mankind and take all of their souls to hell.

There were certainly innocent babies and young children who died in the flood, but the responsibility for their deaths lies upon the heads of their evil parents and Satan, not God, just as the responsibility for Abel's death rested on Cain's shoulders and Satan's, not God's.

Furthermore, the Bible tells us that there are special rewards in heaven for the righteous who die without cause. God has all eternity to make it up to victims such as babies and young children who died in the flood because their parents were wicked, or babies and young children who die of diseases brought upon them by Satan, or the aborted children of our generation who never even make it out of their mother's wombs because of the wickedness of their parents. No, friends. God is not mankind's killer. Satan is.

DID GOD DESTROY THE EARTH?

Even though many of the claims and timelines of modern scientists have been skewed by their foolish faith in the fairy tales of evolution, there are some provable observations in *real* science which are extremely relevant to what actually occurred on Earth before, during, and after the worldwide flood of Noah's day.

From studying the movements of the Earth's tectonic plates over observable history, scientists have reached the logical conclusion that the Earth did not always have the massive mountains and deep oceans which now exist. Neither was the Earth's crust originally shattered into these present unstable tectonic plates which are responsible for earthquakes, tidal waves and volcanoes.

Earth's land mass was once a combination of a single large continent (which scientists call Pangea) surrounded by shallow seas. This is consistent with the Genesis record which indicates that the Earth's outer crust was once a solid surface pushing up through shallow seas, and at that time there were no tectonic plates (the cause of earthquakes, tidal waves and volcanoes).

Do you remember what we discussed? God declared that, in the beginning, everything was "very good". There was nothing at all to cause death and disaster. The fact that many scientists believe that this was the state of the Earth hundreds of millions of years ago is irrelevant because the Bible says they are completely wrong about their time line of Earth's creation and development.

Our modern scientists also know that at some point in the Earth's history, the Earth's climate was sub-tropical right up to the North and South poles. They know this from studying vegetation from core samples obtained in drilling in the ocean floor below the Arctic Ocean which suggest that the Arctic once had a climate similar to Florida. Similar geological drilling in Antarctica indicates that it too was once a sub-tropical paradise.

Scientists have also found sub-tropical vegetation in the stomachs of animals such as mammoths uncovered from the ice in places such as northern Alaska and Russia, and there is fossil evidence indicating that a few Mammoths were still roaming the Earth as late as about 4000 years ago.

Again, this is all very consistent with the Biblical record indicating that at the time of creation, God separated water into the Earth's upper atmosphere to produce a massive water canopy completely enveloping the entire planet to protect it from the ravages of outer space. This created an ecosystem which resulted in a worldwide regulated paradise ecosystem with no extremes of cold at the poles and no unbearable heat at the equator.

In addition, our scientists also know from real scientific observation that at some time during the early history of our planet, the Earth was struck by a number of massive meteors from outer space. The craters from these meteor strikes still remain in several places around Earth and the scientists credit the impact of these craters with extinction level events on Earth.

I repeat, their insistence that this happened millions or billions of years ago is irrelevant because the Bible indicates they are hugely mistaken on the historic timelines of the creation of mankind, Earth, and the rest of the universe. The truth is that the best any scientist can do is to try to imagine the timeline because they were not there when it happened. The Word of the Living God who created all things declares that the Evolutionists are wrong in their misguided opinions, and let's not forget that God WAS there when it happened.

HOW SATAN DESTROYED THE WORLD IN A FLOOD

According to the Bible, our secular scientists are correct in their conclusion that there were ancient meteor strikes which contributed to an extinction level event in Earth's history, but it did not happen billions or even millions of years ago as they imagine. It was one of the first events to occur during the flood of Noah.

People today tend to think of the flood of Noah beginning with a few raindrops and a gentle rain storm, but that is not at all the way it happened. Do you remember that we discussed earlier how Satan is also active in the Second Heaven, always working to try to destroy the rest of the universe that God created?

This is why God is going to create a new heavens and Earth once Satan is permanently deposed. Do you remember where we saw in the book of Job how Satan is the one responsible for ecological disasters, bringing fire down from heaven and blaming God for it? The Bible indicates that Satan is not only the engineer of Earthly disasters. He also produces cosmic ones, and the flood of Noah's day is a good example of this.

The water falling from the sky initiating the flood of Noah's day was no normal rainstorm. It was a worldwide ecological catastrophe of unprecedented proportion. The whole thing was initiated when Satan rained huge meteors down on Earth and they burned and punched so many holes through the Earth's protective water canopy that it began to collapse in a massive deluge of water from the heavens.

Then, once the meteors had penetrated the Earth's atmosphere, they slammed into the Earth's crust with the force of many atomic bombs, shattering the outer and inner crust into tectonic plates and releasing the

Earth's molten core to push the water out from the subterranean aquifers and up to the surface of the planet.

> In the six hundredth year of Noah's life, in the second month, the seventeenth day of the month, the same day were all the fountains of the great deep broken up, and the windows of heaven were opened. And the rain was upon the earth forty days and forty nights. Genesis 7:11-12 KJV

If you remember, Genesis 1 explained to us that, in the beginning, the entire surface of the Earth was covered with water. Then God moved much of the water into the upper atmosphere and more of it into a subterranean aquifer until the dry land appeared. Now, suddenly all of that water was violently being brought back to the surface of the Earth in a short period of forty days until the entire planet was again covered to a depth of 22 feet or more, just as it was at the time of original creation.

> For forty days the floodwaters grew deeper, covering the ground and lifting the boat high above the earth. As the waters rose higher and higher above the ground, the boat floated safely on the surface. Finally, the water covered even the highest mountains on the earth, rising more than twenty-two feet above the highest peaks. Genesis 7: 17-20 NLT

Am I saying that the waters rose so high that they covered Mt. Everest and the Rocky Mountains? Of course not. I am saying that all of these mountains are not as old as the scientists say they are. In fact, they never even existed before the flood. Genesis explains to us that the Earth's topography was high hills (or low mountains-whatever you want to call them), flatlands, gentle valleys, and shallow seas.

The extreme mountains and miles-deep oceans which now cover the Earth are not billions of years old. They rose and descended as a result of tectonic plate movement during the flood. Furthermore, the Bible explains that their formation was a major contributor in the rapid receding of the flood waters from the surface of the Earth after the flood, as were the extremes of cold at the poles and intense heat at the equator. You will see in a few minutes where God's Word talks about all of this:

> And all flesh died that moved upon the earth, both of fowl, and of cattle, and of beast, and of every creeping thing that creepeth upon the earth, and every man: All in whose nostrils was the breath of life, of all that was in the dry land, died. And every living substance was destroyed which was upon the face of the ground, both man, and cattle, and the creeping things, and the fowl of the heaven; and they were destroyed from the earth: and Noah only remained alive, and they that were with him in the ark. And the waters prevailed upon the earth an hundred and fifty days. Genesis 7:21-24 KJV

The flood of Noah's day was indeed an "extinction" level event, a devastating cataclysm which erupted from above and below the Earth's surface with such suddenness and devastating force that no land-based life outside the Ark survived.

Just as it was in the beginning, the flood resulted in the entire world being covered in water to a 22 ft. depth for almost half a year before the planet's new less-than-perfect ecosystem began to stabilize itself into the precarious balance of Earth's present climate zones and weather systems.

Note: We see here that it was only man and land animals who were totally destroyed. Obviously Noah was not able to take aquatic life with him on the Ark, and although much of the aquatic life was destroyed in the deluge, obviously God made provision that there would be enough survivors left to re-populate the Earth again once the waters receded into the rivers and ponds and lakes and oceans that we now have all over the world.

THERE WAS ONLY ONE ICE AGE

Again, the Evolutionists want you to believe that the Earth's history goes back trillions of years, but what do they know, really? They think there was ice age after ice age, death and destruction after death and destruction, but the Bible says that death did not come to planet Earth until Adam brought it. Death came by the actions of one man, Adam, and I tell you by the Spirit of God that anyone who says differently is a liar.

As soon as the Earth's original atmosphere began to collapse, the Earth's poles would have started cooling down and the equator would have started warming up. Within forty days, the Earth's northern and southern poles would have been frozen colder than any temperature on Earth we now experience, and those extreme cold temperatures would have extended all the way down into the areas we know as the temperate regions. It would have been so cold that nothing at all would have been able to survive there at first. Mastodons and other lifeforms at the poles would have been frozen to popsicles where they stood, perhaps even before the flood drowned all of them

Likewise, at the equator and latitudes which now have desert and tropical climates, life would also have been unable to survive. For almost half a year, the heat would have been unbearable, hot enough to boil water and kill anything living. For almost a year, there would have been only one tiny ribbon of habitable space on Earth, the area between the two extremes of hot and cold, and that is where God floated the Ark.

Gradually these two temperature extremes and the seismic activity occurring under the water due to the Earth's crust being broken into volatile tectonic plates began to work together to produce a totally new ecosystem on planet Earth. It would be less perfect, more unstable and far more dangerous than God's original design, but it would become a somewhat functional ecosystem which would enable life on Earth to get a new start.

Once the rain had stopped, and the magma had pressured the broken Earth's crust to push up and fold over in some places and sink down in others, the Word of God tells us that the oceans sank to their present depths and the mountains were pushed up to the majesty we now see until a point of precarious ecological equilibrium was reached.

The two extremes of temperature at the poles and the equator plus the newly formed mountains and oceans also created strong climactic wind circuits to help quickly evaporate surface water into the atmosphere again, forming a new protective "First Heaven" over Earth.

> You clothed the earth with floods of water, water that covered even the mountains. At your command, the water fled; at the sound of your thunder, it hurried away. Mountains rose and valleys sank to the levels you decreed. Then you set a firm boundary for the seas, so they would never again cover the earth. Psalm 104: 6-9 NLT

> But God remembered Noah and all the wild animals and livestock with him in the boat. He sent a wind to blow across the earth, and the floodwaters began to recede. The underground waters stopped flowing, and the torrential rains from the sky were stopped. So the floodwaters gradually receded from the earth…Genesis 8:1-3 NLT

As I said before, regardless of what the Evolutionists claim, here we have the testimony of God's Word telling us that it was during the flood that mountain ranges such as the Alps and the Rocky Mountains pushed up and the deep oceans such as the Pacific and the Atlantic sank down and were formed.

The Bible tells us that Noah was 600 years old when he and his family entered the Ark, and it was a full year later before the waters had receded enough so the land was dried out adequately to enable Noah and his family to leave the Ark and begin their new lives. (Genesis and 7:6 and 8:13).

Satan had done his best to destroy the human race and took many to hell in the process. Maybe there were some who truly repented at the last moment, and if so, God would have saved their souls as they died clinging to trees or the outside of the Ark. We won't know that until we get to heaven.

What we do know is (just like our generation today) Noah's generation had many centuries of warning from God to repent of their sins, but they would not listen, and in the end they all died. Only Noah and his family trusted and obeyed God, and they were the only ones who were spared. God showed mercy on them. If not for God's protection, Satan would have surely killed them too.

NOAH SHOWED GOD HIS FAITH AND GRATITUDE

There were a lot of changes to the world when Noah exited the Ark. But first, Noah immediately showed his gratitude and trust in God by taking some of the extra birds and animals which God had instructed him to take aboard the Ark, and he offered them up to God in a burnt sacrifice, acknowledging that he still realized that his sins needed to be "covered" by the shedding of innocent blood as a reminder that man had brought death into the world.

God was so pleased with Noah and so grieved by what had happened that He declared that never again would God permit everything on Earth to be destroyed for Man's sake. God then told Noah and his family to be fruitful and multiply, and replenish the Earth's human population, and here we are today, all races, creeds and colors on Earth descended from one family, Noah's, all of whom were in turn descended from Adam and Eve, not some troglodyte half-apes, half humans. EVOLUTION IS ALL A LIE.

MAN BECOMES OMNIVOROUS

One of the major changes in the post- flood world was that animals would now have an inherent fear of man, and for good reason. Food was going to be a lot sparser, less nutritious and a lot harder to cultivate in this new less-robust ecosystem. So, God tells Noah that man can add pretty well anything that crawls, swims or flies to his diet.

God then allowed Satan to give the animals a fear of man so they would not all be quickly decimated to extinction before having a chance to reproduce. The only restrictions God placed on man was that the blood must be drained from slaughtered animals before eating them as respect for life being in the blood. God had even instructed Noah from the beginning to take extra pairs of some animals on the Ark because God plans ahead. Those were animals that would be good for food and clothing and more easily domesticated by Noah.

All the animals of the earth, all the birds of the sky,
all the small animals that scurry along the ground, and all

115

the fish in the sea will look on you with fear and terror. I have placed them in your power. I have given them to you for food, just as I have given you grain and vegetables. But you must never eat any meat that still has the lifeblood in it. Genesis 9:2-4 NLT

God also added another stipulation to humanity that modern society has rebelled against, calling it cruel and unusual punishment. I am talking about God's penalty for the taking of human life. God had originally spared Cain for his murder, but now God declared to Noah that it did not matter whether the culprit was animal or human, when a human life is taken in murder, the life of the perpetrator must now be taken as well, as a deterrent to murder.

Anyone who says that swift judgement and capital punishment does not deter murder is a fool. It permanently deters murderers from ever taking another life, and it deters a lot of people from committing murder when they know their own life is definitely going to be taken in retribution. God's Word even tells us that because justice is not carried out fairly and speedily, man's heart is set to do evil. The repeat offenders in our present ponderous justice system are certainly more than enough testimony that God's Word is true and men are liars.

"And I will require the blood of anyone who takes another person's life. If a wild animal kills a person, it must die. And anyone who murders a fellow human must die. If anyone takes a human life, that person's life will also be taken by human hands. For God made human beings in his own image. Genesis 9:5-6 NLT

Because sentence against an evil work is not executed speedily, therefore the heart of the sons of men is fully set in them to do evil. Ecclesiastes 8:11 KJV

I ask you: What has the rejection of the Word of God led to in modern society? Murder is rampant in this generation, and the worst offense is now the murder of multiple millions of innocent children through abortion every year throughout the modern world, something that is a hurtful abomination to God, but now considered to be a legal right and not a crime in the world. I warn you that we are very much closer to the Tribulation and Judgement Day than many people think we are, but that is a book for another day, if the Lord tarries.

THE NEW WORLD AND ITS NEW ECOSYSTEM

The first thing God does in the new ecosystem is to give mankind a Technicolor promise that the Lord will never again permit the entire world to be destroyed with a flood. Now many today scoff at the idea that God created rainbows. They think a rainbow is nothing more than a scientific natural light refraction phenomenon, but God declares that He gave the rainbow to man as a sign of remembrance of what happened in Noah's day because of evil, and a promise from God that it will never happen again.

> Then God said, "I am giving you a sign of my covenant with you and with all living creatures, for all generations to come. I have placed my rainbow in the clouds. It is the sign of my covenant with you and with all the earth. When I send clouds over the earth, the rainbow will appear in the clouds, and I will remember my covenant with you and with all living creatures. Never again will the floodwaters destroy all life. When I see the rainbow in the clouds, I will remember the eternal covenant between God and every living creature on earth." Then God said to Noah, "Yes, this rainbow is the sign of the covenant I am confirming with all the creatures on earth."
> Genesis 9:12-17 NLT

Many people today do not realize that rainbows have not always been with us. Because of the diffused light through the original water canopy and God's testimony that there was no rain before the flood. Noah and his family had never seen a rainbow before they exited the Ark, and neither had anyone else.

117

Do you remember? God's Word revealed to us that before the flood, the Earth was watered with a mist of dew that condensed on the surface of the Earth every night. There was no rain to create rainbows before the flood. The rainbow was a blessing and sign from God that did not appear until after the flood as a promise to mankind that God would never again permit the entire world to be destroyed with a flood of water.

So what has mankind done with God's sign of His mercy? Those who practice every form of evil sexual debauchery in existence have made the rainbow their banner today in direct defiance and rebellion against God. It's really very sad and heartbreaking. However, God was so pleased with His beloved servant Noah that He said:

> And the Lord was pleased with the aroma of the sacrifice and said to himself, "I will never again curse the ground because of the human race, even though everything they think or imagine is bent toward evil from childhood. I will never again destroy all living things. As long as the earth remains, there will be planting and harvest, cold and heat, summer and winter, day and night." Genesis 8:21-22 NLT

There are a lot of things which have changed in this new and less-than-perfect ecosystem which we are now accustomed to, and Satan has had a lot to do with them. Our planet is far more dangerous to life. It is both colder and hotter now, and man cannot survive unprotected in the Arctic and desert regions. We now need protection from the cold or heat during the more drastic seasonal changes. As well, there are now inaccessible mountains and deep, turbulent oceans which are not traversable by humans unaided and unprotected.

The pre-flood generation knew what thorns and thistles and poor growing conditions were like, but they knew nothing of heat prostration or freezing to death. They had never experienced earthquakes, tsunamis, floods, volcanoes, fierce storms, tornadoes, hurricanes, lightning, wildfires and other ecological dangers, not to mention blood sucking disease carrying insects, poisonous creatures and ferocious carnivores.

Man now had a second chance to repent and come back to God after the flood, but this was going to be a new and more difficult existence for humanity. Food was going to be far more difficult to acquire. Disease and infirmity were going to increase to the point where man's lifespan would eventually be decreased to a fraction of what it once was. The average lifespan of man would be reduced to about 70 years, with very few living to 100 or perhaps a little more. To make a long story short, God's protective hedge over mankind was greatly reduced after the flood, and Satan has taken full advantage of it ever since.

God's promise of a Redeemer for mankind was still intact, but the identity of God's Redeemer would not be revealed to mankind until more than 2,000 years after the flood. Now, many centuries later, through the testimony of the Word of God, we can know for a surety in these end times that Jesus Christ is the Redeemer promised to Adam, the Messiah promised to Israel and the Savior promised to the whole world.

In spite of all Satan has done to destroy humanity and our Earth, we now have God's promises to us that whoever repents and believes on Jesus Christ will be saved. So if you are reading this book and have been discouraged with life and fearful about the things that are coming in the future, let me say that God has given us the blessed hope that things will not always be as they are now. Jesus will return to put a stop to all the madness, just as He said He would. Thank you Father God. Thank you Holy Spirit. Thank you Jesus.

CHAPTER 12

Are We In the Last Days?

IS IT THE END TIMES?

Is mankind nearing extinction? Is the end of the world almost upon us? What does the Bible say about the "last days" of humanity? Is there a difference between the last days, the end times and the time of the end? Are we already in the last days? If so, how far along are we? How close are we to the Lord's return for His Body, His Bride? Has the Tribulation started? Will believers have to go through the Tribulation? How close are we to Armageddon, the time when the Bible says there will be a danger of all flesh on Earth being destroyed?

Even among secular scientists and other unbelievers, there are plenty of fear-mongers out there predicting the end of the world and the extinction of the human race. Then, we also have numerous professing Christians doing the same thing. Therefore, many of the questions I have raised in the previous paragraph are on a lot of people's minds today. However, it is not the purpose of this book to spread more doom and gloom. The world already has plenty of that. I believe that God has much better news for those who love Him.

God willing, this is the first of a series of "I Am" books which will be written to help give the reader hope that God is a God of light, love and life. The world needs to know that God has an eternal future for the human race. I hope to help you understand how much God loves us and how much

Satan hates us. I want to help you have the faith to believe that, in spite of how much the Devil hates us and wants to destroy us, God will prevail. In the end, Satan will be vanquished. All evil will be cast into the lake of fire, and all who love Jesus Christ will reign and rule with Him forever.

There's neither the time nor space in this book to go over all the history of man from the flood to the present day. So, let's condense the rest of time between the flood and our present generation down to a couple of paragraphs, and then we will continue on with where our present society is headed, according to the Word of God.

Pretty well as soon as mankind came out of the Ark, most of humanity went right back into sin and false religion again until God slowed the process down by breaking the human race into different language groups.

The Lord did this by confounding man's ability to communicate with everyone else, and this was not an evil thing in itself. Yet Satan used it to breed mistrust, prejudice and hostility between the different language groups. Mankind separated and distanced themselves from one another as they formed smaller groups who spoke the same language as they did. Now motivated by fear of their differences and the inability to communicate, mankind began to spread across the planet as God had instructed them to do in the first place. But now mankind was dividing into different nations and kingdoms, many of which began to develop the goal of world domination and the conquest of other nations.

Later on, as human society continued to grow, just as one man's love of God (Noah's) had found favor with God before the flood, so also, in all of the human race, one man's love of God (Abram's) particularly touched God's heart in the post-flood generation of humanity. Therefore God blessed this man, renaming him "Abraham" and promising him that his descendants would one day become as numerous as all the stars of heaven and they would rule over every nation on Earth.

Now fast-forward about 2000 years. By the time John the Baptist and Jesus come on the scene, we find that even though many of Abraham's descendants still believed in God's promises to Abraham, most of them did not at all have the same love for God that Abraham did.

Therefore, Father God anointed John the Baptist and Jesus to go throughout Israel preaching "Repent, for the kingdom of God is at hand", with John going forth first, declaring that Jesus was the "Lamb of God", mankind's Redeemer which God had promised to Adam and Eve in the Garden of Eden.

So, did those who claimed to be disciples of Moses and children of Abraham believe and obey the teachings of John the Baptist and Jesus? Most of them did not. The end result of John's preaching that Israel's King Herod should abandon his sexual immorality was that John was imprisoned and eventually put to death. Furthermore, the religious leaders of Israel plotted the same fate for Jesus soon after He began to preach the identical message that John had been preaching. "Repent, for the kingdom of Heaven is at hand":

> Now when Jesus had heard that John was cast into prison, he departed into Galilee; Matthew 4:12 KJV
>
> From that time Jesus began to preach, and to say, Repent: for the kingdom of heaven is at hand. Matthew 4: 17 KJV

When Jesus also started teaching that He was the Messiah of Israel, the religious leaders rejected Him. When Jesus began teaching that He was God Himself manifested in human flesh, those same leaders really turned against Him and many actively plotted to kill Him.

There was still a small remnant of believers in Israel who loved Father God and chose to follow Jesus. Yet, history testifies to us that those who hated the light because their deeds were evil, imprisoned, tortured and crucified the Son of God, and in the end, even His closest disciples fled and abandoned Him out of the fear of death, not understanding the whole plan of God.

It was not until Christ rose from the dead and opened their understanding to the Scriptures that the disciples were able to begin to put the whole picture together of God's entire plan for mankind and our Lord's offer of salvation for every one of us.

WHEN DID THE END OF THE WORLD BEGIN?

One thing that we should be grateful for is that the Devil does not know everything. He probably thought that the death of Jesus would be

Christ's defeat. Instead, it was Christ's act of selfless sacrifice to suffer and allow His body to be crucified which ensured Jesus victory over Satan and broke his claim over all mankind.

Christ's willingness to suffer and die without sin for the sake of humanity qualified Jesus to be recognized and accepted by Father God as Adam's Savior. The death of Jesus was the sinless atonement sacrifice acceptable to God for the salvation of every believer in God, right from Adam all the way up to our present day.

Then Father God further honored the sacrifice of Jesus by restoring Christ to His former Glory that He had with the Father in the beginning as the Word of God:

> And now, O Father, glorify thou me with thine own
> self with the glory which I had with thee before the world
> was. John 17:5 KJV

Yes, Father God honored Christ's obedient faith by restoring Jesus to all the former glory and power that He once had with the Father as the Word of God (who was God). This empowered Jesus to forcibly remove all deceased believers imprisoned in the "paradise" realm of Hades within Satan's dominion and take them with Him to the Third Heaven when He ascended to Father God.

Until this time, animals had to be continually sacrificed to cover man's sins. However, the book of Hebrews tells us that Father God was not willing to see His Son continuously sacrificed from the creation of the world for mankind's sins. He would only be sacrificed once without sin to make a way for God to forgive all of mankind's sin through our repentance and faith in Jesus Christ.

The Old Testament system of man repeatedly offering up shedding of blood of animals and covering themselves with their skins was only a temporary atonement for humanity. It was only a shadow of what Christ would do, honored by God until the Son of God, Jesus Christ came to Israel at the "end of the world" to give up His innocent life once to atone for the sins of all who put their faith in Him. Consequently, God's Old Covenant with mankind has now passed away, a spiritual fact that Israel and more than a few professing Christians are still blind to.

> Nor yet that he should offer himself often, as the high priest entereth into the holy place every year with blood of others; For then must he often have suffered since the foundation of the world: but now once in the end of the world hath he appeared to put away sin by the sacrifice of himself. Hebrews 9:25-26 KJV

What we are seeing here is that (in Biblical terms) the beginning of "the end of the world" was initiated by the murder of the Son of God on the cross about 2,000 years ago. The book of Daniel in the Old Testament prophesied of this transference of power and authority from Satan to Jesus many centuries before Christ was even born:

> I saw in the night visions, and, behold, one like the Son of man came with the clouds of heaven, and came to the Ancient of days, and they brought him near before him. And there was given him dominion, and glory, and a kingdom, that all people, nations, and languages, should serve him: his dominion is an everlasting dominion, which shall not pass away, and his kingdom that which shall not be destroyed. Daniel 7:13-14 KJV

It is a truly misleading philosophy to teach that passages in the Word of God referring to the end of the world or the "last days" are talking about the end of existence for all mankind. Although many Christians tend to use the terms interchangeably, even the phrase "end times" has only come into popular use largely as a result of the arrival of many of the modern versions of the Bible which have showed up since the 1960's.

The term "time of the end" appears several times in the KJV of the book of Daniel, and the phrase "end of the world" is spoken of several times in the New Testament, but the words "end times" do not appear at all in the KJV. There's nothing really wrong with the phrase, except that people often misinterpret it to mean that the time is drawing near when humanity will be totally annihilated, and that is simply not true.

More accurately, Bible references to the "last days" and "the end of the world" are describing the last days of SATAN'S RULE and dominion over the human race, as well as the end of this evil world system that we now live and function in. God tells us that Christ died to deliver us from THIS PRESENT EVIL WORLD.

> Grace be to you and peace from God the Father, and from our Lord Jesus Christ, who gave himself for our sins, that He might deliver us from this present evil world, according to the will of God and our Father: Galatians 1:3-4 KJV

Jesus Himself said that the end of the world would not mean the total destruction or extinction of the human race. Rather, it would be a time of judgement and of separation between those who truly love God and those who do not. It is those who remain alive when Christ comes to set up His kingdom, yet try to fight against Him because they do not love God who will be destroyed.

Those who love God and Jesus Christ will reign and rule with Him over the "elect" remnant of mortal believers who will survive the Tribulation in their natural bodies and repopulate the Earth during the Millennium. The wicked will be judged at the end of the Millennium to justify their final destination in the lake of fire, and then when the new Heaven and Earth are created, the resurrected believers will rule with Christ from the New Jerusalem on the new Earth over all mankind for the rest of eternity.

At the opposite end of the spectrum, all those who don't love God will be removed from the kingdom of God so they can continue in their choice to remain under the dominion of Satan, and they will spend the rest of eternity with the Devil and his angels in the fiery domain that God created for the Devil and his Angels.

There will be no cessation of existence. Man was created to live forever. The only choice we have is to decide who we will serve and that will determine where we spend the rest of eternity. Therefore, as we read the Word of God, we should all be thinking about the choices we make in this life, and choose wisely:

> That is the way it will be at the end of the world. The angels will come and separate the wicked people from the righteous, throwing the wicked into the fiery furnace,

> where there will be weeping and gnashing of teeth. Do
> you understand all these things?" Matthew 13:49-51 NLT

Even on the judgement day when the angels separate the wicked from the righteous and the wicked are sent to hell and the lake of fire to be tormented forever, many professing Christians do not understand what is going to happen. They have been taught that it will be the good angels who will do this. Yet, nowhere does the Bible say this.

The pattern that we see over and over throughout the whole Bible is that it is the evil angels whom humanity has chosen to serve who will take the wicked into hell, just as the good angels escort believers to Heaven, and it will be these same evil angels who take the wicked into the fiery furnace with them when they themselves are cast in by Jesus and his armies.

Think about it. The Bible tells us that there will be varying levels of torment in hell just as there will be varying levels of blessing in Heaven. Do you think that it is going to be God or the good angels who will spend their time tormenting the wicked for the rest of eternity? Of course not. The wicked who choose to serve Satan in this life will continue to remain under his dominion for eternity. The only two choices that mankind has is to serve God or serve Satan, and the choice made in this life extends into eternity.

We see from Scripture then, that when the Bible speaks of the end of the world, it is not talking about human extinction, but about the end of this present world system which is ruled by Satan and dominated by evil. In the Bible, "the end of the world" is referring to the segregation and eternal banishment of those who now choose to serve Satan and the Antichrist over God and Jesus Christ.

But doesn't the Bible talk about the heavens and the Earth being burned up and completely consumed in fiery judgement? Well, yes it does indeed, but this is not so God can destroy all of humanity, as many are teaching.

This creation of a new heavens and Earth will not occur for another thousand years after Christ puts an end to Armageddon and sets up His kingdom on Earth. It will happen at the end of the Millennium. After Satan has been released from prison at the end of the Millennium, he will try and fail one last time to use the remnant of mortal humanity to overthrow Christ. After that final attempt, Satan and all who follow him will be cast forever into the lake of fire and God will then create a completely new heavens and Earth.

While the wicked certainly have a fearful looking forward to coming judgement, the eventual dissolving of this corrupted universe is something that we should be looking forward to because this entire present universe has been damaged by evil and Satan's presence in the Second Heaven, the First Heaven and Earth. It all presently exists upon thousands of years of death and destruction. Therefore God is going to dissolve it all before He remakes a new heavens and Earth in order to make all things "very good" again and eternally suitable for the sons and daughters of God to inherit:

> But the day of the Lord will come as unexpectedly as a thief. Then the heavens will pass away with a terrible noise, and the very elements themselves will disappear in fire, and the earth and everything on it will be found to deserve judgment. Since everything around us is going to be destroyed like this, what holy and godly lives you should live, looking forward to the day of God and hurrying it along. On that day, he will set the heavens on fire, and the elements will melt away in the flames. But we are looking forward to the new heavens and new earth he has promised, a world filled with God's righteousness. 2 Peter 3:10-13 NLT

> And I saw a new heaven and a new earth: for the first heaven and the first earth were passed away; and there was no more sea. Revelation 21:1 KJV

As far as the "last days" goes, Abraham's grandson Jacob (whom God renamed "Israel" and became the patriarch of the nation of Israel) prophesied about the last days and Israel's coming Messiah:

> And Jacob called unto his sons, and said, Gather yourselves together, that I may tell you that which shall befall you in the last days Genesis 49:1 KJV

> Judah, thou art he whom thy brethren shall praise: thy hand shall be in the neck of thine enemies; thy father's children shall bow down before thee. Judah is a lion's whelp: from the prey, my son, thou art gone up: he stooped down, he couched as a lion, and as an old lion; who shall rouse him up? The sceptre shall not depart from Judah, nor a lawgiver from between his feet, until Shiloh come; and unto him shall the gathering of the people be. Genesis 49: 8-10 KJV

The name "Shiloh" means peace or tranquility and it is one of the epithets or descriptive names for the Messiah. So, who is this Messiah who will finally bring peace to Israel and the rest of the World? Who is this old lion, this ruler of Judah whom Jacob is talking about? The Word of God clearly tells us who it is:

> For unto us a child is born, unto us a son is given: and the government shall be upon his shoulder: and his name shall be called Wonderful, Counsellor, The mighty God, The everlasting Father, The Prince of Peace. Isaiah 9:6 KJV
>
> The next day John seeth Jesus coming unto him, and saith, Behold the Lamb of God, which taketh away the sin of the world. John 1:29 KJV
>
> And there shall be no more curse: but the throne of God and of the Lamb shall be in it; and his servants shall serve him: Revelation 22:3 KJV

How sad it is that (just before the crucifixion of Jesus Christ) one of the questions Pilate asked the leaders and people of Israel is "Shall I crucify your king?" (See John 19:15). Pilate finally gave into their demands, but insisted on nailing a sign to the cross saying "Jesus of Nazareth, the King of the Jews".

The religious leaders unsuccessfully petitioned Pilate to have the sign changed to "he said he was king of the Jews" because they did not believe Jesus was their king. Yet Pilate refused, so the sign remained as an everlasting testimony to what had been done. What a tragedy this was and still is, and how fickle mankind can be. When Jesus had entered Jerusalem only a few days earlier, this was the welcome He got:

> On the next day much people that were come to the feast, when they heard that Jesus was coming to Jerusalem, Took branches of palm trees, and went forth to meet him, and cried, Hosanna: Blessed is the King of Israel that cometh in the name of the Lord. John 12:12-13 KJV

The Apostle Peter did not mince any words about the backslidden state of his nation, and about what had happened in Israel. Listen to Peter's first message on the Day of Pentecost after Jesus Christ's resurrection:

> "So let everyone in Israel know for certain that God has made this Jesus, whom you crucified, to be both Lord and Messiah!" Acts 2:36 NLT

Yet wicked leaders continued to turn the people against God and against Jesus, just as many in Israel and around the world still do throughout mankind today. But do not despair, dear friends. God works all things together for good. During his writing of the Book of Revelation, the Apostle John was caught up in the spirit to the Third Heaven and this is one of the things that He saw:

> And I wept much, because no man was found worthy to open and to read the book, neither to look thereon. And one of the elders saith unto me, Weep not: behold, the Lion of the tribe of Judah, the Root of David, hath prevailed to open the book, and to loose the seven seals thereof. And I beheld, and, lo, in the midst of the throne and of the four beasts, and in the midst of the elders, stood a Lamb as it had been slain…Revelation 5:4-6 KJV

Yes, dear friends. Jesus Christ is the Lion of the tribe of Judah. He is the root of David destined to rule the Earth and the entire of creation forever, and He is also the Lamb of God who was slain for our redemption and reconciliation back to Our Father God who lives in Heaven.

CHAPTER 13

The Wicked Demand Signs

THE LAST DAYS HAVE ALREADY BEGUN!

That's right. Beloved friends. Just like the "END OF THE WORLD", the "LAST DAYS" began when Jesus Christ showed up in Israel two thousand years ago, and these last days have been building to a climax ever since that day. The people before the flood were wicked. The people of Sodom and Gomorrah were violent and wicked. The people who crucified Jesus were wicked.

The people of Nazi Germany were desperately wicked, murdering over 6 million Jews, and being responsible for initiating a war which eventually led to the deaths for between 60-80 million people. Yet, none of these were as evil as our present society has become.

Never mind the false imprisonments, tortures, murders, wars, starvation, and deaths from diseases and ecological disasters going on all over the world. Never mind all of the other evils that are occurring daily all over this planet. In our generation, recorded statistics are indisputable proof that every year now over 40 million innocent children are being murdered worldwide through abortion alone.

I am telling you by the Spirit of God that our loving Father in Heaven is not going to allow this horrendous level of evil against His offspring to go on much longer. Our generation has filled the cup of evil almost to the brim. In early human history, God abhorred pagans who offered their children as sacrifices to false Gods. Yet, our modern society is doing the exact same thing, and to an even greater level, and the prophets of God are warning mankind that God is about to remove the last of his protection from this present generation very soon.

We are now entering the midnight hour of the last days. The wicked will continue in their wickedness, mocking and laughing at the prophets of God, calling evil "good" and calling good "evil" and saying "Where is the promise of His Coming?" But we who love the Lord know that the return of Jesus is much closer than most people believe.

Jesus Christ is the Lion of the tribe of Judah, the King of Israel, the Lamb of God, and the Savior of the Gentiles, and, just as He said He would, very soon Jesus is coming again for those who love and believe in Him:

> Let not your heart be troubled: ye believe in God, believe also in me. In my Father's house are many mansions: if it were not so, I would have told you. I go to prepare a place for you. And if I go and prepare a place for you, I will come again, and receive you unto myself; that where I am, there ye may be also. John 14:1-3 KJV

> God, who at sundry times and in divers manners spoke in time past unto the fathers by the prophets, Hath in these last days spoken unto us by his Son, whom he hath appointed heir of all things, by whom also he made the worlds; Who being the brightness of his glory, and the express image of his person, and upholding all things by the word of his power, when he had by himself purged our sins, sat down on the right hand of the Majesty on high: Hebrews 1:1-3 KJV

There you have it. The Word of God indicates to us that the "last days" began with arrival of Jesus Christ on Earth, and the time referred to as "the end of the world" began when Jesus gave His life on the Cross for mankind's salvation.

In the Book of Acts, the Apostle Peter also confirmed to us on the Day of Pentecost that the last days have already begun. Furthermore, another sign God has given that this is true was the arrival of the Holy Spirit and the formation of the church on the Day of Pentecost shortly after Jesus Christ's Resurrection:

> But this is that which was spoken by the prophet Joel;
> And it shall come to pass in the last days, saith God, I
> will pour out of my Spirit upon all flesh: and your sons
> and your daughters shall prophesy, and your young men
> shall see visions, and your old men shall dream dreams:
> And on my servants and on my handmaidens I will pour
> out in those days of my Spirit; and they shall prophesy:
> Acts 2:16-18 KJV

ARE THERE ANY OTHER "LAST DAYS" SIGNS?

Jesus gave us many. The increase in wickedness, the increase in ecological disasters, the increase in sexual deviance, the increase in violence, the decrease in fair law and speedy execution of justice. However, there is one major sign that many people don't want to believe, one that even many professing Christians seem to be blind to. It is the worldwide resurgence of false religion, including the false religion of Evolutionism.

Yes, I repeat that belief in evolution is not a science. There is no sound scientific evidence at all to support society's blind belief in the vain imaginations of Evolutionists. Yet, Hollywood and educators and scientists and politicians and yes, even religious leaders are all grooming our generation to believe that the false theories of evolution are true, and the Word of God warns us that this would be a major sign that we are in the last days before Christ returns for His Bride:

> For the invisible things of him from the creation of
> the world are clearly seen, being understood by the things
> that are made, even his eternal power and Godhead; so
> that they are without excuse: Because that, when they
> knew God, they glorified him not as God, neither were
> thankful; but became vain in their imaginations, and
> their foolish heart was darkened. Professing themselves to

be wise, they became fools, and changed the glory of the incorruptible God into an image made like to corruptible man, and to birds, and four footed beasts, and creeping things. Romans 1: 20-23 KJV

Remember how we discovered from 2 Peter 3 that these are those who walk after their own lusts and scoff at the idea that there was ever a worldwide flood.

It is important that we think carefully about these passages of Scripture, because God is not just talking about the superstitions of heathen nations who worship their ancestry as snakes or monkeys or birds or sea creatures or animal-human hybrids or imaginary human like gods such as Zeus and Odin and such. The Bible is also talking here about people believing lie of the false religion of evolution which declares that man is genetically evolved from such creatures and came into being independently of God.

It is The Evolutionists who care nothing for God and God's goodness. They don't believe in the God of the Bible. They don't believe we need God and they are deceiving the people by telling them that we do not really need to follow God. They preach that if mankind works hard, we can save ourselves and our planet. They think that if we continue to increase our knowledge, we will one day move out into the stars, colonize the moon and other planets and ourselves evolve into gods or god-like beings, all independently of the one true God who created us.

Evolutionism is nothing new. It is an old, old lie of Satan cloaked in modern language and pseudo-scientific terms. The Devil has enlisted all kinds of helpers to make evolution more convincing. He now utilizes geologic timetables, Hollywood, space age computer graphics and misguided world leaders, school teachers and unlearned preachers to make evolution seem believable, but listen to me, dear friends.

It is still idolatry. It is still all smoke and mirrors. It is the same old lie that Satan presented to Adam and Eve in Genesis in the Garden of Eden. "Believe what the Devil says, and follow the Devil, and you shall be as (evolve into) gods."

THE ABSENCE OF NATURAL AFFECTION

The other major "sign" which God has given us to warn that our present society is in the midnight hour of the last days is the sign of absence of "natural affection" in modern human society.

This term is very important to understand, but it is only used twice in the Bible (once in Romans 1 and once in 2 Timothy 3), and both times the phrase is included in a long list of symptoms of the sinful and corrupt society which will exist during the last days, a society which will be marked by rampant sexual immorality and deviance.

Let me give you a Biblical definition of what natural affection is. Natural affection is the "real" goodness and love that God implanted within man's nature when man was first created. It is love for God above all else, the same kind of love He has for us. It is loving our fellow man as much as we love ourselves, and this starts with loving our spouses, our siblings, our children and our parents and then spreads to everyone else we come in contact with.

God created mankind the way that He did because the Lord desired to have family. God wanted to bear His children through humanity. Our Father in Heaven wanted us to perpetually reproduce children in His image and His likeness throughout the universe ad infinitum, forever. That is why God created the tree of life. Man was not created to die! It was God's desire that man would eat from the Tree of Life and continue to live forever.

On the other hand, Satan has always hated God's plan from the very beginning because he knows that one day mankind will rule over him and banish him to the lake of fire forever. Consequently, it has been Satan's goal all along to try to put a stop to human reproduction. Satan has always wanted to kill man. His goal is to kill every adult human being and every human child and every baby that he can get away with. Just take a look at the historical record in the Bible and you will see that I am right.

Satan took full advantage of man's long lifespan before the flood. He continued to deceive mankind and turn humanity against God until (within a very few generations) natural affection was all but eradicated from the entire human population of Earth. By the time Noah reached adulthood, the whole Earth was filled with violence, sexual immorality, and demonic infatuation.

Undoubtedly, if not for God's protection, the wicked of Noah's generation would certainly have killed Noah and his whole family. Eventually, evil reached a level where God said "No more!" and the Lord took His protection away and allowed Satan to destroy all but Noah and his immediate family with the flood.

CHAPTER 14

God is Light, Love, Life

GOD DOES NOT HATE US!

I do realize that sexual sin has been a sensitive topic and I really hope you are still with me because I want to re-emphasize to every reader that no matter what our sin has been, God does not hate us. He does not condemn us, but He does hate the evil that we do because God hates how evil destroys His children and robs us of the light, love and life that God wants to give us.

In the beginning, God created the Earth and made it come alive by utilizing God's own personal light and warmth. Then God transferred some of that light to the sun, moon, and stars, all for the benefit of, and in preparation for the creation of God's children. Contrary to what the Evolutionists teach, the universe was not created first, it was created after the Earth for humanity's benefit.

God says the universe was created for the marking of time and for signs and seasons and so that man would never be in total darkness, even when the Earth turns away from the sun, and once humanity had filled the Earth, I believe that it was God's desire that the human race would continue to expand out into the rest of the Galaxy and beyond.

How it all started for humanity was that God took some of His light, His love and His life and fashioned a spiritual being, a son created in God's own image and after God's own likeness. Calling the man Adam,

God made a biological body for Adam from the very same elements of which the Earth itself is made, and because Adam was created sinless in the very presence of God, Adam was filled with the Holy Spirit, clothed in glory brighter than the sun, and everywhere Adam went, the glory of God shone from him to light his path. In the beginning, mankind did not need material clothing, for the glory of God was their covering.

Then God created a life companion and helper for Adam. Using biological material from Adam's own body and manipulating the genetic components, God altered the DNA so that Adam's companion would be female. That way, together mankind would have the ability (through the union of man and woman) of creating temples (biological bodies) to house every new child of God who would come into existence.

Think about it, friends. God loved mankind so much that He gave us the blessing and wonderful honor to be able to participate with God in the creation of every human being in existence. How much do you think it hurts God then, when millions of His children are being killed in this generation through the horrendous evil of abortion, man murdering God's offspring? The terrible sin of abortion is an abominable crime against God, and may just be the primary reason that the judgement of God is ready to fall on this end times wicked and adulterous generation.

Nonetheless, our Father in Heaven still loves us. It broke the Lord's heart when Adam and Eve rejected Him and turned away from Him. Yet it was not God who killed Adam and Eve by gradually corrupting and destroying their perfectly created biological bodies. It was evil. It was Satan, but even in the death of our bodies, God has shown us mercy.

DEATH IS OUR RELEASE, NOT OUR CURSE

Satan is still wandering around lying today, and because of that, most people on Earth have the truth backwards. The Devil wants you to believe that evil is good and death is a vengeful God's curse upon mankind. No! No! No! The truth is just the opposite of that. Evil is the curse (from Satan) that is destroying mankind, and God has ordained that death is the limit of which the curse of evil can harm all who want to come back into God's family again.

God only drove mankind out of the Garden of Eden so that they would not be able to eat from the Tree of Life and be doomed forever with evil continuing to torture and corrupt their bodies and being for all eternity, for God declares to us in Mark 9 that hell is a place where their worms do not die and the fire is not quenched.

Even though God's beloved children had rejected their Father and joined Satan against God, the Lord did not abandon mankind. Rather, God allowed death to come to humanity so that mankind would not end up like Satan and the Angels, continuing to live forever with no good in them. Instead, God gave man a mortal lifespan and the hope of a Redeemer who would be born of Eve's offspring, promising that one day mankind's Savior would crush Satan's hold over humanity.

During Old Testament times, God gave the opportunity for humanity to be saved by "grace through faith" in God's promise of a coming Redeemer. All throughout history, from Adam to the thief on the cross, the way of salvation announced by God through His prophets was "Repent (for forgiveness of sins) and Believe on the coming Redeemer of mankind (for salvation)."

When Abraham came on the scene, God promised Israel that the Messiah and Savior of the world would come out of Israel from the Tribe of Judah and be born in Bethlehem, but until then, right up until John the Baptist identified God's Savior as Jesus Christ, the message of the way of salvation remained the same for humanity. "Repent and believe on God's coming Redeemer." Then through the Spirit of God, John the Baptist gave humanity the new revelation that "Jesus Christ" was the Lamb of God who takes away the sin of the world.

THE PREACHING OF REPENTANCE

There are many professing Christians today who are in denial that repentance is still an essential requirement for mankind to be saved, confusing the preaching of repentance with the false concept that we can be saved by our good works.

Yes, Jesus Christ is the Redeemer whom all of mankind has been waiting for, and He is the One in whom we must believe, for there is no other name under heaven whereby mankind can be saved. Yet, the only change that has been made to God's way of salvation since the arrival of Jesus Christ has been for God to identify who the Savior is.

As Peter and all the other disciples preached throughout the New Testament, the way of salvation for mankind is still the same "Repent and believe on the Lord Jesus Christ", and anyone who thinks that they can continue in their evil ways while professing to be a Christian is going to be in for a very shocking surprise when the Spirit and the Bride are gone and the door to Heaven has been closed again, and they are among the many who will be left behind.

Dear friends, do you want to know the true definition of the false doctrine of "salvation by works?" That is when people think that they can go on disobeying God and practicing iniquity in this life, and God will accept and honor their charitable works, or religious service, or proclamations that "Jesus is Lord" in spite of the fact that they are continuing in direct disobedience to God in their daily behavior. To these, Jesus will say "Depart from Me all who work iniquity. I never knew you."

Let's all be wise, beloved. God is only calling us to repentance because it is the evil that is destroying us. Yet, in so many cases (through our continued evil behavior) we retain our enslavement under Satan's dominion and the one thing that God will not do is override mankind's free will. As long as the majority of the human race continues to reject God and insists on following the Devil in spite of all of God's warnings, evil will continue to dominate and worsen in our present world.

However, God's Word tells us that we are not to be troubled by this as those are who have no hope, because God has given us a blessed hope. Jesus promised that before the Antichrist comes to power and the worst arrives, Jesus, the Bridegroom will return to Earth to choose a Bride, and we are almost at that day now. Yes, I know there are some who say that God is going to require Christ's beloved bride to go through the tribulation and then be raptured at the end of it all, proclaiming that they are ready to suffer through it all and die for Jesus. But is that what Christ is going to demand of those He loves?

Even though the righteous do suffer in this life, God declares that the wrath of God is not for the righteous, but for the wicked, and for those who say that the wrath of God does not begin until the second half-of the tribulation, they are being willingly ignorant that God says in His Word that literally billions will die during the first half of the tribulation in the 4th seal judgement and the 6th trumpet judgements alone (Revelation 6:7-8, Revelation 9:13-19) and millions more will be killed by many other causes.

For those who say that this is only the wrath of Satan, not the wrath of God, who are you kidding? Listen to yourself. Billions will die because the wrath of Satan is the wrath of God. God does not do this stuff, even though the Lord accepts responsibility for it happening. The whole Tribulation is the work of Satan.

The idea that God's beloved Bride will go through the whole Tribulation and then be raptured at the end of it all is even more unbiblical. After more than half of the world population has already been killed before the middle of the Tribulation, God explains to us in Revelation 9 why the Tribulation will continue for another three and a half years:

> And the rest of the men which were not killed by these plagues yet repented not of the works of their hands, that they should not worship devils, and idols of gold, and silver, and brass, and stone, and of wood: which neither can see, nor hear, nor walk: Neither repented they of their murders, nor of their sorceries, nor of their fornication, nor of their thefts. Revelation 9:20-21 KJV

> But let us, who are of the day, be sober, putting on the breastplate of faith and love; and for an helmet, the hope of salvation. For God hath not appointed us to wrath, but to obtain salvation by our Lord Jesus Christ. 1 Thessalonians 5:8-9 KJV

So we see, just as I said before, the Tribulation and the wrath of God is reserved for the wicked, not the righteous. Jesus has not appointed His beloved Bride to wrath.

JESUS WILL CATCH UP THOSE WHO LOVE HIM

You can call it the "blessed hope". You can call it the "catching up" of the Bride of Christ. You can call it the first "resurrection". You can call it the "Rapture". It does not matter what we call it. What matters is that Jesus said it will happen, and all of the signs are pointing to the reality that it is going to happen very soon, when the whole world and many in the church are least expecting it:

> And now, dear brothers and sisters, we want you to know what will happen to the believers who have died so you will not grieve like people who have no hope. For since we believe that Jesus died and was raised to life again, we also believe that when Jesus returns, God will bring back with him the believers who have died. We tell you this directly from the Lord: We who are still living when the Lord returns will not meet him ahead of those who have died. For the Lord Himself will come down from heaven with a commanding shout, with the voice of the archangel, and with the trumpet call of God. First, the believers who have died will rise from their graves. Then, together with them, we who are still alive and remain on the earth will be caught up in the clouds to meet the Lord in the air. Then we will be with the Lord forever. So encourage each other with these words. 1 Thessalonians 4:13-18 NLT

Are you ready for this? Are you ready to go with Jesus when He comes? Is Jesus really "Lord" of your life? Or are you going to continue to practice the kind of evil behavior which testifies you are still following Satan (regardless of whether or not you say you are a Christian).

Yes, I know that there are those who say the church must go through the wrath of God to the middle or end of the Tribulation and then be raptured. We've already talked about those who love the Lord not being appointed to the wrath of God, but there several other Scriptural reasons why the Rapture will not occur at the end of the Tribulation.

We have just read in the Scriptures that during the Rapture, Jesus will not actually come all the way down to Earth. The heavens will be opened and Jesus will call for those who love Him to come UP. That is the first key. When Jesus returns to call His Bride, we will be going UP with Jesus to go to His Father's House, and so shall we ever be with the Lord from that moment on.

However, when Jesus returns to put an end to Armageddon at the end of the Tribulation, God tells us in His Word that the saints will be coming DOWN from heaven WITH Jesus. Speaking of a prophecy that goes all the way back to Enoch, the great grandfather of Noah, Jude tells us that the judgement of the wicked will end with the Lord returning with His saints.

> Enoch, who lived in the seventh generation after Adam, prophesied about these people. He said, "Listen! The Lord is coming with countless thousands of his holy ones to execute judgment on the people of the world. He will convict every person of all the ungodly things they have done and for all the insults that ungodly sinners have spoken against him." Jude 1:14-15 NLT

There is a lot more that can be said about this, but to avoid a 500 page book, I will only mention one more important fact from Scripture. The Word of God is quite clear that (sadly) during the seven year tribulation, almost everyone left on Earth after the Rapture will die.

Jesus said that if He does not return to put a stop to it, there would be no flesh at all left alive. But for the sake of a small elect remnant of believers whom God will use to repopulate the Earth during the Millennium, Jesus and the saints will return to slay the rest of the wicked and set up Christ's kingdom on Earth as it is in Heaven.

So when Jesus returns to Earth at the end of the Tribulation, there will only be two classes of people left in the world. There will be the wicked who will be slain at Christ's appearance (Revelation 19:21) and there will be the elect, the small remnant of Tribulation saints whom God will protect until the end of the Tribulation for the purpose of repopulating the Earth again during the Millennium.

Exactly how many that will be, we don't know. The Bible does not say, but I doubt that it will be the multitudes portrayed by Hollywood. Let's not forget that God only needed 8 people to repopulate the Earth the first time. The more important point is that there will only be these two groups of people left alive at the end of the Tribulation. Everyone else will be dead, so there will be no one else left living to be raptured, so the Rapture will definitely not be happening then.

Listen to what I am saying, dear friends. We must not be deceived into continuing in our wicked ways, unwisely thinking that we will "get right with God when we see the sign of the Antichrist. By then it will be too late. Now is the time for Repentance. Now is the time for believing in and obeying Jesus Christ.

God has declared to us that the unrepentance of this wicked and rebellious generation is soon going to take mankind from under God's protection and open up the world to seven years of Great Tribulation under Satan's wrath because (when the Rapture occurs) the Devil will know his time of dominion over humanity is almost over.

> Therefore rejoice, ye heavens, and ye that dwell in them. Woe to the inhabiters of the earth and of the sea! for the devil is come down unto you, having great wrath, because he knoweth that he hath but a short time. Revelation 12:12 KJV

I hope that this book has helped you to see who our real enemy is, past, present, and future. I also hope you are beginning to understand that, even though the Bible does speak of the Great Tribulation as being the wrath of God, it is actually, the wrath of Satan which God is going to allow to be unleashed in these last days on a wicked and unrepentant generation.

God does not want this to happen, but because God does not want any to perish, He WILL allow all this to happen in order that (after finding out how truly terrible the consequences are of becoming a servant of evil are) there will be some who will finally come to the truth during the tribulation and turn back to God and be saved, like branches snatched out of a fire.

Let us remember, friends. God did not bring death into the world, Satan did, and death will be the last enemy to be vanquished when Jesus returns. God did not kill Adam and Eve. God kept Adam and Eve alive for many centuries so that they could bring forth many generations of offspring and pave the way for the Redeemer of all mankind to be born. Only when they had reached a ripe old age did God reluctantly allow Satan to take their lives

Enoch walked with God and pleased God so much that Father God could not bear to see Satan kill him, so He removed Enoch and took him to Heaven without dying as a shadow of the coming resurrection of the Bride of Christ. No, God did not destroy the world with a flood. God (through Enoch, Methuselah and Noah) actually warned mankind to repent for centuries because judgement was coming. But when they would not listen, God set apart and protected the only people left on Earth who still loved and served him, and removed His protection from all who preferred darkness over light, evil instead of good, and let the destroyer Satan do what he does and take their lives.

God was not the one who sent evil bands to steal kill and destroy in Job's life. God did not send fire and tornado to torment Job and kill his children. God did not afflict Job with a loathsome disease. God did not do any of it. Satan did all of this evil, so stop saying that God does these things to test and teach us and build our faith.

Yes, God took responsibility for the destruction of Sodom and Gomorrah, but it was not God who rained down fire from the sky upon the wicked. God was the one who sent in his angels to warn the righteous to get out before Satan would be released to destroy everything and then take the wicked to hell.

When Jesus and the disciples were in the boat, it was Satan who sent the storm to destroy them and God who calmed the seas.

It is not God who has brought suffering and persecution upon Israel and upon Christians, even though God does take responsibility for it. This is the work of Satan, who hates the people of God. Yes, God removes His protection from people and whole nations for a time, but not for their punishment and destruction. Rather, that once they come to realize how cruel and evil a master Satan is, they might come to repentance and return to their loving Father in Heaven and not be lost forever.

Now, here we are in the end times, even the last days. We are close to the end of the world as we know it. Satan is about to be cast down to

Earth in a great rage and God does not want any of us to go through the coming Tribulation, the last seven years of hell on Earth before Satan is bound and removed from the Earth.

God is our Eternal loving Father in Heaven, and as the title of this book declares, He loves us deeply. We are all like prodigal children who have all strayed far from God and it does not matter where we have gone or what we have done, God wants us to turn around, turn away from our wicked ways and come back to Him.

God wants our ears to be tuned to hear the trump of God and the angels' call to COME UP, because the Bridegroom is returning for us. Jesus does not want us on Earth to live through seven years of destruction and death. God wants us to be ready and have the light within us to see the way to the open door of heaven, so that we may go through it when it opens.

Like Enoch, God wants to spare us from the judgement that is coming by taking us up to Heaven, and that will be a matter of God's timing, not our worthiness if we are alive when the rapture occurs. It will not be because we deserve it, but because He loves us and it pleases Him that we love Jesus and have chosen to follow Christ rather than Satan.

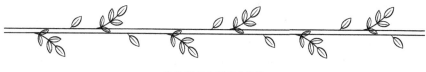

CONCLUSION

In closing this book, let me reinforce that God loves each and every one of us, and wants us all to come back to Him, but it is up to us individually to decide whether or not we want to do that. We are all prodigals and we need to decide if we are going to believe and heed God's warnings about the final and eternal destiny of the wicked. Or (like the people of Noah's day and the people of Sodom and Gomorrah) are we going to decide to continue in our evil ways which will lead to our own destruction and eternal torment in the presence of Satan, the one whom we have chosen to follow.

Listen to the Spirit of God, dear friends. The preaching about Jesus coming for those who love Him is not a scare tactic. It is a comforting promise and a hope that we who love Jesus Christ are eagerly looking forward to. Before Jesus left, He said:

> "Don't let your hearts be troubled. Trust in God, and trust also in me. There is more than enough room in my Father's home. If this were not so, would I have told you that I am going to prepare a place for you? When everything is ready, I will come and get you, so that you will always be with me where I am. John 14:1-3 NLT

I am not perfect. No one is. I still fail God at times. We all do, and it should grieve us enough when it happens to convict us to repent and get back on track with God again.

More than anything, I want Jesus to come back so that we can all be finally rid of our fallen flesh that has become corrupted. I truly want the knowledge of evil totally eradicated from my being so that not even the memory of it exists anymore and all that remains in my being is the goodness of God forever.

Come quickly Lord Jesus so that all of your children subject to corruption can put on incorruption. We long for the day when we mortals will put on immortality and join you in our Father's home in heaven until the appointed time for you to bring us back and establish your eternal kingdom on Earth as it is in Heaven.

Until that time, let your Holy Spirit guide us, purify us and strengthen us to walk ever more closely with you as we continue to do our best to follow Christ in this life, calling others also to come out of darkness and into the eternity of God's light, His love and His life through Jesus Christ, our Savior.

And I pray that all the people can say "Amen!"

OTHER BOOKS BY MICHAEL HUNTER

Dangerous
Journey
Home

The author's own testimony of how Jesus Christ
saved him and changed his life forever.

See preview and ordering information on the following pages.

After 30 years of ministry,
Okanagan pastor tells his own story in his book

An illegitimate son born of a Scottish immigrant born into family dysfunction, PTSD, abuse, violence and kidnapping.

Early years marked by depression, rage, guns, motorcycles, drug and alcohol abuse, pornography, illegitimate sex, and searching unsuccessfully for happiness and fulfillment in life.

Then - a life-changing encounter with God initiated a sincere nine year search for God in all the wrong places, a sinful and dangerous journey which ended in financial ruin, shame, divorce, maximum security prison, and the verge of suicide before again encountering God and finally coming to an understanding of how much Father God really loves us and wants us to come back into His arms of love.

Today we live in perilous and uncertain times and Jesus warned us that in the last days many people would be troubled with fear, depression and hopelessness, but there is hope. This is one man's story of how God is a forgiving and merciful God, a God of second chances and new beginnings, and all God is asking of us to to turn to Him with all of our hearts.

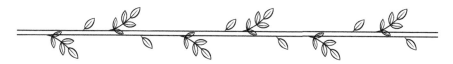

ABOUT THE AUTHOR

Pastor Michael Hunter has been involved in teaching and prophetic ministry for more than 35 years. He has been a member of the Christian Ministers Association of Canada since 1987 and presently functions as an associate pastor at: Lake Country Life Center in British Columbia, Canada.

Printed in the United States
By Bookmasters